EXPLORING FABRIC PRINTING

'PRAY be careful to keep the Book clean, the Patterns have cost a deal of Money, and are easily Spoiled by children, or Careless Persons putting their hands on them; it is therefore hoped and entreated, that the utmost care will be taken to sully the Patterns as little as possible, and when any Lady sends for a Sight of the Book it is entreated she will give Orders that it be Returned immediately.'   From a bound sample book, Carlisle, 1780–85

By the same authors:
(published by Mills & Boon)
Simple Fabric Printing
Advanced Fabric Printing
Exploring Puppetry

By Stuart Robinson:
(published by Studio Vista)
A History of Dyed Textiles
A History of Printed Textiles

(published by Visual Publications)
sets of transparencies of historic
dyed and printed textiles with notes.

EXPLORING
FABRIC
PRINTING

STUART and PATRICIA ROBINSON

With drawings by the authors
and title pictures by Sheila Robinson

MILLS & BOON LIMITED, LONDON
CHARLES T. BRANFORD COMPANY, USA

Dedicated to Tom Corbin, who, as a member of the Inspectorate, did so much to arouse interest in fabric printing as a school craft.

British ISBN 0 263 51391 2
American ISBN 0 8231 7021 7

© 1970 Stuart and Patricia Robinson

First published 1970 by Mills & Boon Limited,
17–19 Foley Street, London W1A 1DR

First published 1971 by Charles T. Branford Company
Newton, Massachusetts 02159, USA

Printed and bound in Great Britain by Bookprint Limited, Crawley, Sussex

Every care has been taken to check the recipes and materials recommended in this book. Local differences in water, atmosphere and working conditions can have minor effects on printing or dyeing and where possible such variations have been allowed for.

CONTENTS

General source books
dealing with Textile Printing
of all types.

*Note—Specialized bibliographies and
suppliers of materials appear at the end
of the appropriate section as listed above.*

ACKNOWLEDGEMENTS

We are most grateful to the many students and teachers who by practical experiments and valuable suggestions both in colleges of education and with children in schools have tested the methods and recipes in this book.

In particular, we would most sincerely thank our colleagues Muriel Somerfield who took a number of photographs and Hetty Wickens for her ready help in the section on natural dyes; Dr P. Quensel and S. Napier, editors of *CIBA Review*, for their unfailing courtesy and the loan of a number of illustration originals; CIBA-Clayton Ltd, Manchester and Leicester, Hoechst Cassella Dyestuffs Ltd, Manchester, and Imperial Chemical Industries Ltd, Dyestuffs Division, Manchester, for technical advice; Susan Bosence, fabric printer of Dartington; Margaret Hoather of Birmingham College of Education; Mrs Anne Maile; Noel Dyrenforth; Mary Frame; Michael O'Connell; Rita Martin; Elizabeth Tate; Barbara Wolstenholme and students of Coventry College of Education for permission to use examples of their work as illustrations; and the following for help in one way and another:

Robert Armstrong Collection; Christiansens Diamond Products; Department of Information, Djakarta; Edinburgh Weavers; Grant Collection, U.S.A.; Heal Fabrics Ltd; James Howard Collection; Hull Traders Ltd; Liberty of London; Macclesfield Engineering Co. Ltd; Veronica Marsh; Möllnlycke Hemtextil, Sweden; Musée de l'Homme, Paris; Museum of Ethnology, Basle; Museum of Fine Arts, Boston, Mass.; Museum of Applied Arts, Zürich; G. W. Pearce & Sons Ltd, Birmingham; J. Redgrave; Sanderson Fabrics Ltd; H. Steiner Collection; Trustees of the British Museum and the Ethnographic Department in particular; UNEEK, Edgware Road, London; The Victoria and Albert Museum and in particular the Department of Textiles, the Indian Section and the Circulation Department.

INTRODUCTION

'We should have nothing in our houses which we did not either know to be useful or believe to be beautiful.'
William Morris c 1870

'All living things yearn for colour.'
Goethe

In common with 'Exploring Puppetry' and other books which are being planned, 'Exploring Fabric Printing' aims to provide ideas and techniques for creative work. In particular it deals with the quick production of decorated fabrics using, in the main, only the simplest equipment and methods. It is written for the amateur as well as the more experienced craftsman.

In the past, the most successful techniques for fabric printing were highly specialized and hidden in the literature of the textile chemist. The dyes often required elaborate processes and varied chemicals to fix them on the cloth. In addition there was the prevalent attitude that all craftsmen had to follow a long apprenticeship of set rules before they could achieve results which then had to conform to a given convention.

The craft, as a craft, was the most important consideration. Nowadays the techniques are often considered to be subordinate to the experience and to the final results of the craft. This attitude, together with the development of more permanent dyestuffs and simpler recipes, has brought textile design and decoration within the reach of all.

In particular, it is the change in attitude that now prevails towards all art and craft teaching that has encouraged a more liberal approach in the individual crafts.

In fabric printing this has led to the recognition that it is much better to allow ideas and patterns to develop on the fabric rather than to attempt to make the design on the textile conform exactly to a preplanned painted design upon paper. Too often such treatment means that the resultant pattern does not appear as an integral part of the fabric but rather as a superimposed decoration. It remains a design worked out in one medium and merely transferred without adjustment to another.

Just as crafts involving clay, metal, plaster or wood cannot be learnt entirely from books or at a drawing board, so the craft of fabric decoration must arise from the use of the materials themselves. The fabric, the threads, the textures and the dyestuffs must be constantly used with an open mind as far as the end result is concerned. Fabrics are exceedingly versatile: they can be used flat, folded or draped. But, whichever way they are used, the design, if it is true to the nature of the fabric, will seem to be an integral part of the material.

Dyestuffs fall into two main categories. Firstly, the transparent and translucent dyes which, whilst colouring and staining the fibre, still allow it to show through. Secondly, the pigment dyestuffs that coat and hide the fibre just as paint covers and hides the wood of a door. The quantity of dyes available is almost numberless but many are unsuited to the hand craftsmen since they demand far too complicated machinery and a high degree of skill in their preparation and use. Fortunately, this still leaves a great many dyes which can be used with the simplest apparatus in a normally equipped room and which will give excellent results including high fastness to light and washing. Since certain classes of dyestuffs react better with certain types of fibres it will be seen that the same dye may work well with one fibre, only give paler shades on a different one and not work at all with yet another. This point we have indicated in the text and set out in the recipes and factual notes for quick reference.

The very fact that the hand craftsman cannot hope to achieve as perfectly matched repeats as can the machine is his greatest strength. It enables him to build up new ideas, modify previous conceptions and switch from one technique to another as and when he feels this necessary. His work will develop a rhythm of tying or printing and this will gradually become as insistent and complex as rhythm in the dance or music. Each form of printing has its own particular 'feel'. The wise craftsman therefore does not try to imitate the particular effects of batik or tie and dye with a screen, for each technique dictates its own way of working and, within its limits, each can be most rewarding and satisfying.

Each section starts with a general introductory paragraph about the particular dye or method of dyeing, gives a list of the equipment needed, describes the methods of working, suggests simple experiments as well as some further more involved ones and finally concludes with a note on reference material. It is hoped that the ideas presented here will serve as a source of inspiration and not merely as ideas to be imitated. For this reason, only the very minimum of instructions have been given so as to allow entirely original results to be achieved.

The illustrations have been selected to show the work of children, students, craftsmen and professionals.

TAKE CARE

Certain dyestuffs (e.g., Pigment dyes) contain small amounts of petroleum products or other inflammable solvents. So use in a well ventilated room, away from naked flames, and not whilst smoking.

Some chemicals used in fabric printing are mild poisons or are corrosive. Therefore these should be stored under lock and key and kept in labelled, screw-topped jars.

Particular care is required when making solutions of sulphuric acid or caustic soda. In either case the chemical *must be added* to the water for, if water is poured on either substance, great heat will be generated and burning splashes thrown several feet.

If the skin is splashed with any corrosive, flood the afflicted place at once with cold running water. Hold a splashed eye open under cold running water for a few moments and refer to a doctor at once. Keep a First Aid box in the room and see that it is kept well stocked.

GENERAL WORKROOM PRACTICE AND INFORMATION

One of the many advantages of fabric printing as a school craft is that most of the techniques described in this book can be carried out with scrap materials and normal household equipment and chemicals such as salt and soda. Expensive apparatus is not necessary and one can improvise using common objects.

Serious printing however demands the careful planning of the workroom and certain basic equipment like:
(1) a flat table top
(2) a source of heat (gas ring or multi-heat electric ring)
(3) space for drying (clothes horse or lines)
(4) a steam iron
(5) a small portable convector heater
(6) a nearby sink

It is an advantage to have the heat source near to the sink and the sink near to the printing table which is best situated in a position which allows working from all sides.

The first essential is any large, heavy, well-made bench with a level top (Figure 1). This could be a kitchen table or one especially constructed from Dexion or Handy Angle. The printing surface is prepared by covering the table top (or the frame construction) with a flat surface made in one piece.

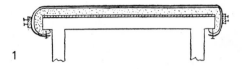

On a 1-in. table top made from level planks, preferably tongue and groove jointed, a covering of 1 piece of $\frac{1}{8}$-in. hardboard will be sufficient. If the top is at all uneven (e.g., made from loose planks) or where a frame only is available, the covering surface should be made from one piece of $\frac{1}{2}$-in. or thicker chipboard, blockboard or plywood as sold by timber and builders' merchants in sheets 4 ft. wide by varying lengths up to 12 ft. This top should be glued and screwed or bolted to the existing table top or frame (screw or bolt heads countersunk and plugged level) and the corners and edges smoothed down with sandpaper.

Stretch one or two layers (without joins or mends) of blanket, carpet underfelt or $\frac{1}{4}$-in. foam underlay over the table top. On top of this layer stretch one piece of heavy plastic sheeting (Marley film is excellent) or the special plastic waterproof covering sold for fabric printers by such firms as the Macclesfield Engineering Co. Ltd (so-called American oil cloth soon wears out and is not recommended for hard wear).

It is preferable to fix these layers down if this is at all possible with strips of wood along or underneath the edges of the table. The finished table must be rigid, have a perfectly level top and yet 'give' a little during the printing.

VERY APPROXIMATE PROPORTIONS AND EQUIVALENTS

All *level* spoonfuls (GB).

1 teacup	=50 teaspoonsful	=18 dessertspoonsful	=12 tablespoonsful	
1 breakfast cup	=68 teaspoonsful	=22 dessertspoonsful	=15 tablespoonsful	=$\frac{1}{2}$ pint
1 tablespoonful	=3$\frac{1}{2}$ teaspoonsful	=1$\frac{1}{2}$ dessertspoonsful	=approx. 1 oz	=28·50 gms
1 dessertspoonful	=2$\frac{1}{2}$ teaspoonsful			
1 imperial pint	=20 fluid oz	=20 oz avoirdupois	=0·567 litre	
1 imperial gallon	=160 fluid oz	=10 lb avoirdupois	=4·545 litres	
1 litre	=34 fluid oz	=2 lb 2 oz avoirdupois	=1·759 pint	
50 new pence	=$\frac{1}{2}$ oz approx.	=13·5 gms		
10 new pence	=$\frac{1}{2}$ oz approx.	=11·31 gms		
5 new pence	=$\frac{1}{5}$ oz approx.	=5·66 gms	single coin	
2 new pence	=$\frac{1}{4}$ oz approx.	=7·12 gms	piece	
1 new penny	=$\frac{1}{8}$ oz approx.	=3·56 gms		
$\frac{1}{2}$ new penny	=$\frac{1}{16}$ oz approx.	=1·78 gms		

$$\text{lbs per imperial gallon} = \frac{\text{grams per litre}}{100}$$

$$\text{ozs per imperial gallon} = \frac{\text{grams per litre}}{6·25}$$

grams per litre $= 100 \times$ lbs per imperial gallon
grams per litre $= 6·25 \times$ oz per imperial gallon
Centigrade to Fahrenheit $=$ Multiply by 9, divide by 5, add 32
Fahrenheit to Centigrade $=$ Subtract 32, multiply by 5, divide by 9
Boiling Point of Water $= 100°C. = 212°F.$

1 oz Dye powder	= 14 teaspoonsful	1 oz Nafka Gum Crystals	= 4 teaspoonsful
1 oz Urea	= 8 teaspoonsful	1 oz Solution Salt SV Crystals	= 10 teaspoonsful
1 oz Resist Salt L powder	= 16 teaspoonsful	1 oz Caustic Soda Flakes	= 6 teaspoonsful
1 oz Calgon powder	= 9 teaspoonsful	1 oz Formosul powder	= 7 teaspoonsful
1 oz Manutex Gum powder	= 10 teaspoonsful	1 oz Glauber Salts Crystals	= 7 teaspoonsful
1 oz Sodium Bicarbonate powder	= 6 teaspoonsful	1 oz Sodium Phosphate Crystals	= 5 teaspoonsful
1 oz Anhyd. Sod. Carbonate powder	= 13 teaspoonsful	1 oz Washing Soda Crystals	= 7 teaspoonsful
1 oz Common Salt	= 8 teaspoonsful	1 oz Alum. Chrome Crystals	= 7 teaspoonsful
1 oz Brentamine Fast Black K Salt	= 8 teaspoonsful	1 oz Ammonium Oxalate Crystals	= 7 teaspoonsful
1 oz Tapwater	= 7 teaspoonsful	1 oz Ammonium Bichromate Crystals	= 8 teaspoonsful
1 oz Sodium Chlorate	= 4 teaspoonsful	1 oz Potassium Bichromate or Dichromate Crystals	= 5 teaspoonsful
1 oz Sodium Acetate	= 4 teaspoonsful		
1 oz Sodium Chlorate powder	= 4 teaspoonsful	1 oz Shellac Flake	= 18 teaspoonsful

NOTE: Please remember that these are only approximate equivalents.

COMMON NAMES

Soda Ash   is the commercial name for Anhydrous Sodium Carbonate
Potash   is the commercial name for Anhydrous Potassium Carbonate
Common Salt   is the commercial name for Sodium Chloride
Glauber Salts is the commercial name for Sodium Sulphate
Washing Soda is the commercial name for Sodium Carbonate

A description such as 'Ammonium Nitrate 1:1' means a solution of ammonium nitrate in its own weight of water and so on—for any chemical described in this manner.

A simple working top to keep on the table when not printing is a useful luxury (Figure 2).

2

It is of course quite feasible to keep the *table* top as the general working surface and prepare the printing surface on a very rigid, loose cover.

A trolley, small table or shelf is useful for mixing dyes, etc., and an ironing board, a kettle, saucepans, measuring jug, plenty of newspaper and rag, bowls, spoons, soft scrubbing brush, a few assorted paint brushes, and greaseproof or tracing paper are all necessary equipment.

Dyes, chemicals and thickeners should be kept in screw-topped containers in a lockable cupboard away from all direct heat.

USEFUL INFORMATION

1. **Always** mix dyes over newspaper.
2. **Always** use a clean, dry spoon for each dye or chemical.
3. Replace the lids, stoppers, corks, etc., on dyes and chemicals *immediately* after use.
4. **Always** stand the dye pad on newspaper when printing.
5. Gum and most mixed dyes (except Procion M) should keep for a few days *in a cool place*; some keep much longer.
6. **Always** put the **name of dye** (e.g. Procion Blue H3GS) and the **date** made or the **type of gum** and the **date** made, on the side of bowl. Cover with newspaper or card to store and keep in a screw-topped jar for long storage.
7. Recipes throughout are in parts, e.g., *level* spoonful. The same spoon must be used throughout each recipe. (A heaped spoonful can contain anything from 2–4 times as much as a level spoonful.)

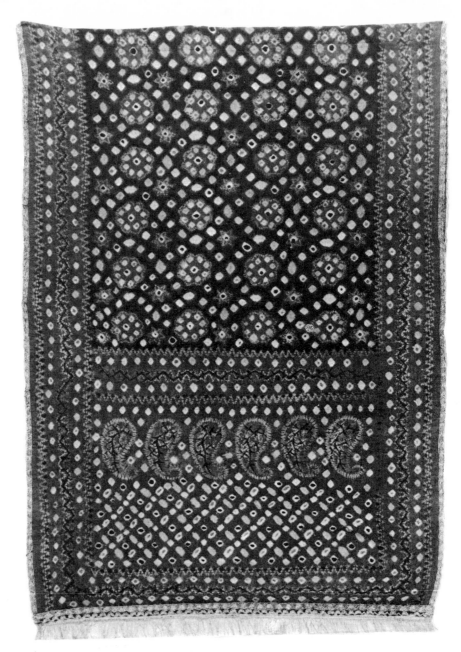

3A   Silk shawl from Palembang, Sumatra, folded in half. The ornaments are tied to give white, yellow, orange, red, blue, green, and purple against a brownish-red ground. *Courtesy Museum of Ethnology, Basle and CIBA Review.*

TIE AND DYE

This is one of the oldest forms of pattern making on cloth, it is a 'resist' technique in which, before dyeing, parts of the fabric are knotted, tied up with thread, string or raffia, or sewn and the thread drawn up.

Known also as 'plangi' (Malay), 'band-hana' (India), and 'shibori' (Japan), Tie and Dye was once wide-spread in all parts of the world except Oceania and Australia. It was particularly developed in India, Indonesia, China, Japan, West Africa and parts of the Americas.

Although at times factory-produced imitations of tie and dye and batik have been attempted, these are usually very inferior both in design and finish. This is due not so much to the difficulty of imitating the patterns as to duplicating the quality of chance which is always present in the repeat of a hand-produced fabric. This accidental quality is what has always endeared these crafts to the craftsman. A number of present-day craftsmen carry on the craft and include Anne Maile, Mary Frame (Mrs Carrick of Tie and Dye Ltd) and Patricia Robinson.

3B   Cotton fabric from Bombay State, displaying plangi designs. Four layers of folded material are patterned at the same time, thus producing four identical motifs. The colour of the ground is red and the patterns appear white or yellow. *Courtesy Museum of Enthology, Basle and CIBA Review.*

Tie and Dye requires the very minimum of apparatus and can be done by anyone —children, students, amateurs, invalids or, of course, at an advanced craftsman's level. The knotted, tied or sewn portions of the fabric resist the dye in varying degrees depending upon the tightness of the knot or tie. These 'resisted' parts remain the original colour of the material. Further tying will 'resist' other portions, or the previous ties may be undone to allow a second colour to take over the original fabric colour. In this manner the most complicated and original patterns may be evolved from relatively simple techniques.

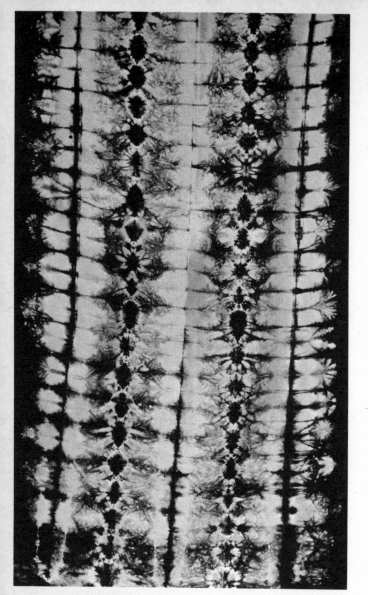

4 Tie dye showing a series of ties in one colour combined with pleats in a second colour—*Patricia Robinson*.

SOME SIMPLE EXPERIMENTS

You will require some thin white or tinted cotton fabric (such as old handkerchiefs, pieces of old sheets, pillow cases, calico, muslin, poplin or cambric) or old plain silk scarves, linen, fine wool or viscose rayon.

Two kinds of dyes may be used:
(1) Dylon hot water dyes which will require salt, saucepans and some dye mixing bowls, which will withstand heat, i.e. not plastic ones.
(2) Dylon cold water dyes which may be used with any kind of bowl or large jam jar as no direct heating is necessary. Salt and washing soda are used with these dyes. Procion M dyes may also be used cold (recipe pages 32 and 139).

In both cases spoons, scissors, warm water, etc., will also be required.

For the actual ties you will require white or natural thread, natural raffia, and fine white or natural string for fine to medium fabrics. For heavy fabrics one can add natural string or twine to above list.

When sufficiently patterned and dyed, the fabric is rinsed in cold water and the ties removed. At this stage it is important not to cut the fabric itself whilst cutting the ties. To avoid doing this use small, thin-bladed scissors. The blade is inserted under a thread and this one thread is then cut. The remainder of this particular tie can then be easily unravelled and removed (Figure 4). Then the full design is revealed as a light pattern against a dyed background. An alternative form is described on page 26 where a coloured pattern is obtained on a light ground by a discharge or bleach method.

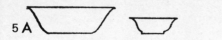

5   A—Wide based bowls are safer in use than narrow based bowls; B—Use two wooden sticks or spoons when stirring tie and dye to keep the fabric moving and so obtain even dyeing.

A sheet of asbestos or an asbestos mat under the gas or electric ring is a sensible precaution. After dyeing place a half-filled bowl of cold water very close to the saucepan and transfer the fabric to it with sticks. Rinse well in a bowl or a sink. Dye left in the saucepan can be used again but will give a much paler shade than the first dyeing; C—Cut the thread very carefully with small thin bladed scissors; D—Lie flat on paper on floor or hang out to dry.

Folding and knotting (Figure 6)

Take a large piece of white cloth about 2 in. square and fold (A). Pick up by the centre point and allow the cloth to hang in folds (B). Smooth into a long, thin rope (C) and make a fairly tight knot as near to the point as possible (D). Next, make normal knots at each corner (E).

Take another, similar piece of cloth, wet it and repeat knotting as above but with only two corners tied (F).

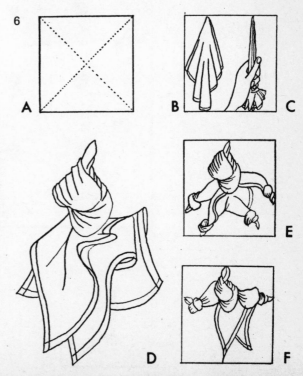

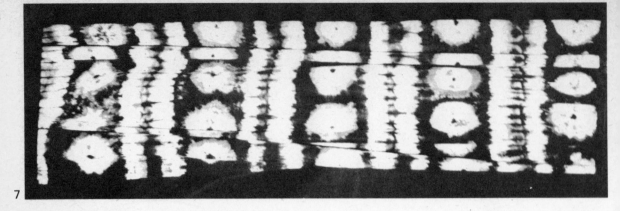

7

Prepare the dye according to the maker's hand method instructions given with each dye tin, wet *both* tied fabrics and place both in the dyebath and dye according to the instructions. Remove from the dye, rinse in cold water, squeeze out and leave to dry. Upon unknotting, the 'resist' effect of the knots will be seen as well as the difference between wet and dry, and tight and loose knots (Figure 7).

7 An example of circular ties and pleated ties on a Chlorazol Black E200 dyed cotton fabric.

8 A—Creases on an old handkerchief shown by dotted lines; B—Ties with thin thread at points marked * in A. They should be tied around about six times up and down and then knot; C—Use a thicker thread at ● tying around about nine times up and down and then knot; D—Use thin string or raffia to tie the central point ■ with several ties with $\frac{1}{4}$ in. space between; E—The method of tying. Leave an end tie up to point, down on top of previous tie and knot.

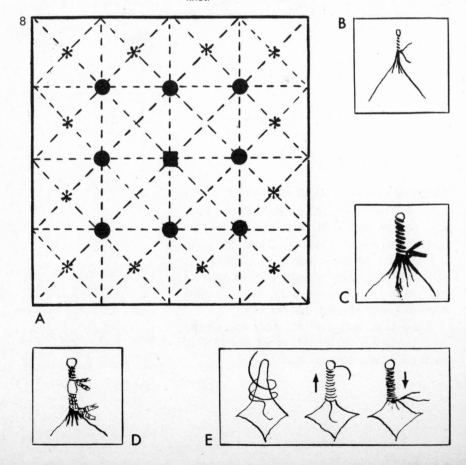

Ties with thread (Figure 8)

Crease an old handkerchief (A) and open out on the table. Use a thin thread to tie outside dots (as shown by *), a thicker thread to tie middle dots (shown by ●) and thin string or raffia to tie the centre point (■). In each case tie fairly tightly. Wet cloth, and dye as before. Rinse, dry, carefully untie and iron out flat.

The difference in the patterns resulting from different threads—string and raffia—will be clearly shown as well as the bands of tying.

9 Circular ties as in Figure 8 showing centres tied with coarser string, outer circles with medium thread.

B

Ties with buttons, seeds, etc.
(Figure 10)

Various objects can be tied into the fabric
(A) and give most unusual results. Avoid
tying too tightly or the fabric may split
during the dyeing particularly with seeds
—lentils, peas, beans, barley, corn, etc.,
that swell in water. Other objects that can
be used include beads, buttons, cotton
reels, pieces of wood, corks. Several different objects may be tied in any one fabric
but it is important to mark out the fabric
with creases, leaving room between buttons, etc., to allow the fabric to wrap
around each object. Always work from the
centre outwards, for if you tie the outside
first it is exceedingly difficult to control
those ties and still correctly place the
inside ties. Where a continuous row of

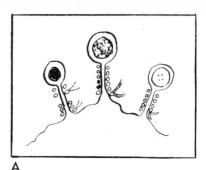

A

10

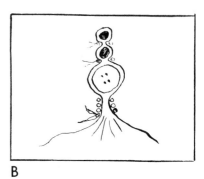

B

11 Section of a silk shawl
patterned with various designs
produced by inserting beads,
stones, wood pieces and binding below each as described
in Figure 9. In this example the
ground is green, the patterns
purple, crimson, yellow and
white. It is probable that the
colours within the large squat
diamonds were applied with a
brush. Produced on the Island
of Lombok, Indonesia. *Courtesy Museum of Ethnology,
Basle and CIBA Review.*

objects is to be tied into the fabric use a continuous thread from one object to the next with a slip knot behind each object.

A series of objects may be tied in, one above the other (B).

Objects such as corks or pieces of wood dowelling may be bound around with thread after being tied into the fabric (C).

C

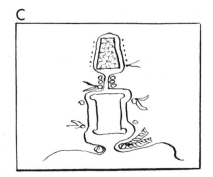

Gathered Ties (Figure 12)

This is a development of the last form. The fabric is wrapped around a piece of circular or square dowelling (A) and then tightly gathered to one end and trapped with very tight diagonal ties (B). This can be done by sliding along the smooth dowelling or by previously inserting threads and pulling these up (C). This amount of tying will give an end strip of border pattern on a plain background (D). A second tying at the other end will give a border at each end with a plain colour between (E). The rod or rods are stood in the dyebath with the cloth end in the dye and the wood standing out (F).

12

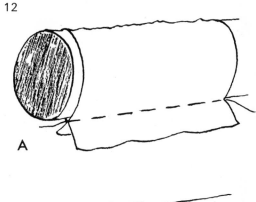

A

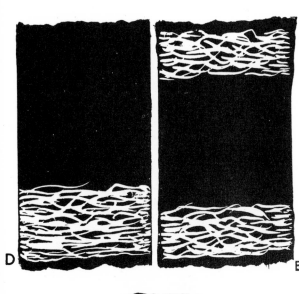

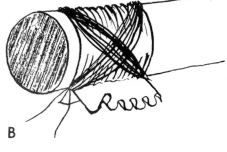

D   E   B

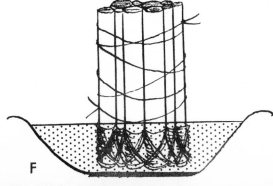

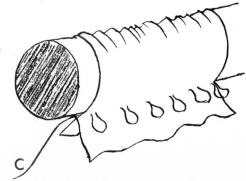

F   C

FURTHER WORK IN TIE AND DYE
Pin tying to give spots of colour
(Figure 13)

To tie and leave a spot of colour, insert a fine pin or needle as near to the point required as is possible (A). Stroke the fabric down into even folds and tie with a fine thread right up to the pin. If a band of resist is required tie a little more than the required width (B and C).

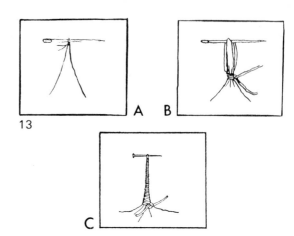

13

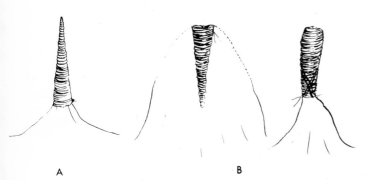

A   B

Complete resist to give a large undyed area (Figure 14)

Tie an end on the wrong side of the fabric (A). Turn this tie inside and completely enclose this first tying with a second tie on the right side of the fabric (B).

14

Random texturing (Figure 15)

Make a ball of waste cloth or newspaper and wrap the fabric around it without undue overlap. Bind very tightly with thread in all directions until the whole ball is very tightly tied up. After dyeing in the usual manner and untying, the fabric will be heavily textured. It can be used as a background to further regular pattern ties or other forms of decoration such as Batik, Screening, Potato or Scrap printing, or Embroidery. This process may be done by making a ball of the fabric itself without a paper or cloth ball inside and with normal tying only.

15

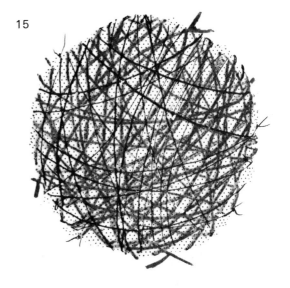

Pleating or folding to give stripes
(Figure 16)

The fabric may be pleated in length, tied around with thread, raffia or string at intervals (A) and then dyed, untied in part, further ties added, and redyed as required (B). Take care to do a zig-zag pleat and not to hide parts by wrapping around.

An even simpler way is to fold once in the direction of the eventual stripes, pleat up, tie and dye (C). See that the pleats are opened out during dyeing. Further ties and dyeing can then be added.

It will be seen that a variety of different stripes can be produced if the first fold is 2, 3 or 4 or more folds (D).

It is also possible to tie across the first tie for the second dyeing (E).

16

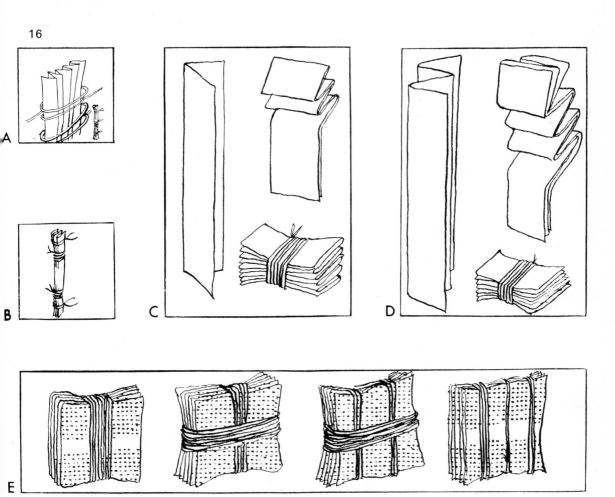

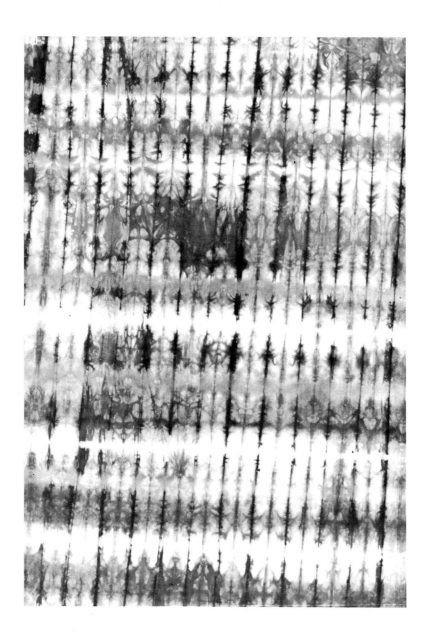

17 An example, in two colours of a pleated and tied length as described in Further Work page 21. *Patricia Robinson.*

Square patterns (Figure 18)

A large variety of patterns may be produced by the simple folding of the square in different ways and some are shown here.

18 Square patterns. A—a—fold a large plain handkerchief into four; b—fold corners to centre: c—fold down centre to leave corners exposed; d—tie, dye, rinse, retie etc. as required. B—a—fold into four and on diagonal to form a triangle; b—fold over twice; c—tie, dye etc. C—a—fold as before; b—tie two or three corners, dye etc. D—a—fold with outside corners to each side; b—tie, dye etc. E—a—crease on dotted lines; b—tuck in sides as shown; c—press flat; d—zig-zag pleat one side to centre line, taking care to keep even, level sides; e—zig-zag other side; f—fold back to back as shown; g—tie, dye etc.

23

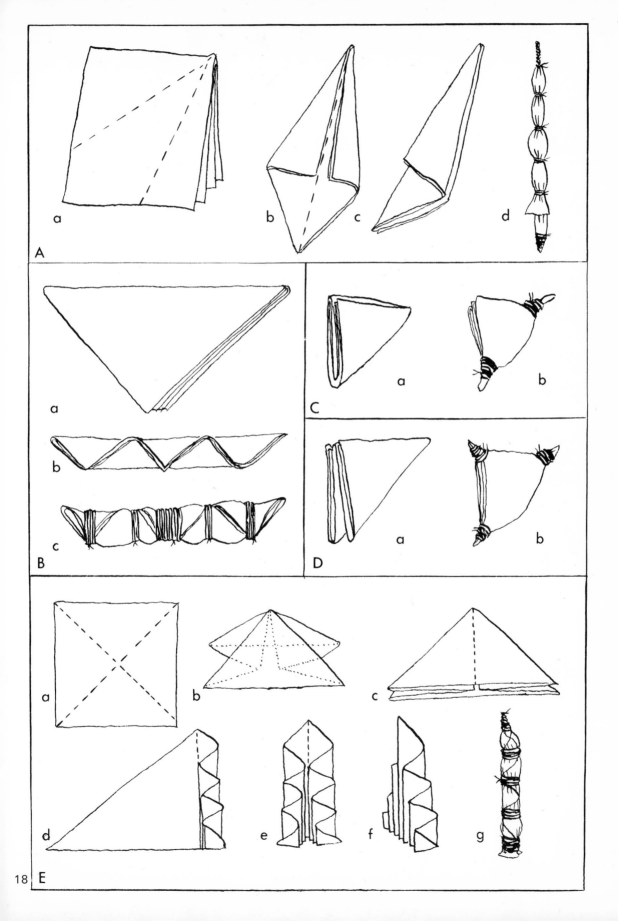

18

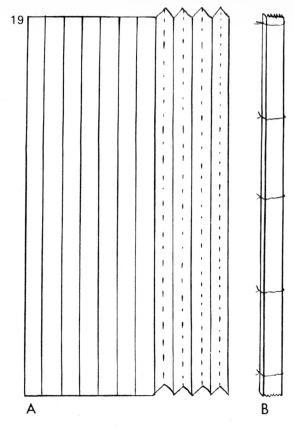

19

A

B

Rope and pleated ties (Figure 19)

Again the fabric is pleated (A), loosely bound in order to hold it in place (B), tied (C), then dyed etc., as before.

All these ties may be made from diagonals (D–F) or they may be folded over and tied in a variety of ways (G).

NOTE—The following two methods require a shorter time in the bath.

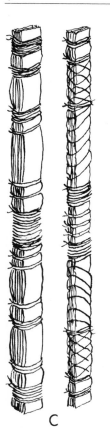

C

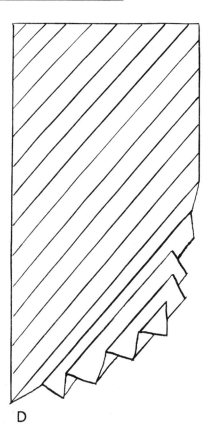

D

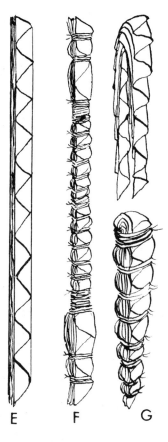

E

F

G

Sewing or tritik (Figure 20)

In this method a strong thread, such as linen carpet thread, is sewn into the fabric with a running thread (knotted at loose end) which is then drawn up tightly and fastened off firmly with two or three over-stitches to keep the fabric drawn up securely together. It is essential to knot before and after drawing up. If the thread gives during dyeing the pattern will be spoilt.

As will be appreciated there are many different ways of using this tritik method and a number are shown here. It is a most effective form of patterning and has been used with infinite variety in most parts of the world where Tie and Dye has been extensively practised. It is still used in West Africa and parts of South and South-East Asia.

20 Sewn or tritik patterns A and B—lines of resist may be formed by putting up one or more running threads with a knot, at both ends; C—a number of stripes folded together and sewn together; D—a sewn and drawn up spiral to give E. F—edge or fold oversewing.

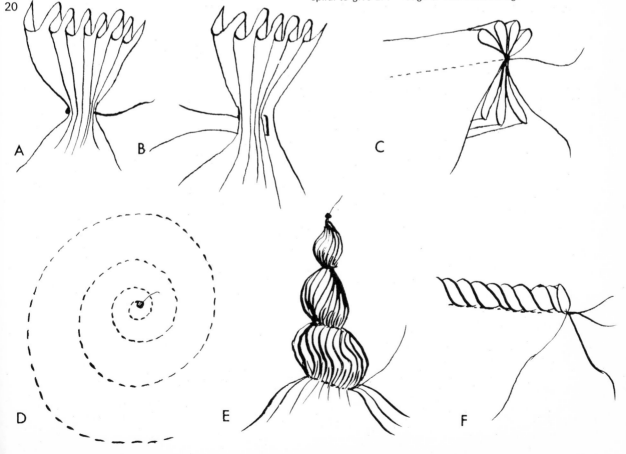

21A An indigo dyed, stitched design (tritik) upon a European brocaded cotton cloth produced in Senegal, W. Africa early this century. *Courtesy of the Trustees of the British Museum.*

22 Tie dyed fabric from the Baule tribe on the Ivory Coast. Design shows white on a light blue ground. *Courtesy Museum of Ethnology, Basle and CIBA Review.*

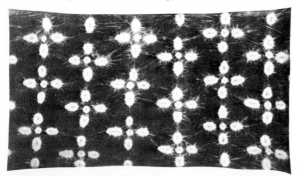

GENERAL NOTES

1. The type of tie used must be suited to the thickness of the fabric. Fine materials such as muslin and lightweight silks and poplins may often be folded double and then tied as a single fabric.

2. It is essential to mark out the pattern in some way before commencing the tying, as the first few ties will distort the fabric beyond recognition and make regular tying impossible unless the pattern is marked. A small, faint dot from a soft pencil is quite sufficient. Allow space between dots for the fabric taken up by the ties.

3. As with Batik it is possible to work on fabrics with an existing self or printed stripe or dot pattern as long as the manufacturer's dye will stand your own dyeing.

4. Tie and Dye may be practised with all types of dye except Pigment dyes (such as Polyprint, Tinolite, Printex, etc.). The tied fabric may be steamed if the dye requires it, without protective wrappings.

5. Where two or more dyes from the same class of dye are mixed in the same dyebath and this mixture is used to dye the tied fabric, it will be found that one colour will travel further under the ties than the other colour or colours. This will give a halo around the white resist left after the ties have been untied.

Discharge tying (Figure 22)

This method involves dyeing the cloth a plain, even colour *before* it is tied and with a dye which can be bleached out *after tying* to either white or a paler shade of the dye colour.

The cloth is first dyed all over to an even colour, then tied as required, or knotted or sewn or any combination of previous methods and placed in a bath of bleach. This can be Dygon or a very mild household bleach (e.g., 1 part bleach—6

21B   Sewn and drawn up shape.

parts of water). Do not use too strong a solution since this will rot the fabric. Rinse thoroughly after bleaching out. With this method the ties appear in colour and the background is pale or white.

Many variations of texture and depth of discharge are possible and dyed fabrics can be tied, discharged, and then tied and dyed in the normal manner.

SUPPLIERS OF TIE DYE MATERIALS
In addition to the firms mentioned in the general list of suppliers. (Fabrics—see page 151; Dyes, page 123.)

Great Britain
Candlemakers Supplies—101, Moore Park Road, London, S.W.6.
Dryad Handicrafts—Northgates, Leicester, for raffia, Dylon dyes, cottons, fabrics.
Dylon Hot and Cold Water Dyes—Chemists, Hardware, Multiple stores, (request a leaflet on how to use) or from Mayborn Products Ltd, Dylon Works, Sydenham, London S.E.26.

USA
Tintex dyes are obtainable from most department stores and supermarkets.

FURTHER SOURCES FOR MORE ADVANCED TIE DYEING
Apart from the books mentioned in the General Bibliography the following are also recommended:

Tie-and-Dye as a present day craft by Anne Maile, Mills and Boon, London, 1970.

An excellent, comprehensive and very well-illustrated standard work by an experienced practitioner of the craft.
CIBA Review No. 104 'Plangi Tie-and-Dye' by A. Buhler, The Editors, Ciba Review, Basle, Switzerland.

A standard monograph upon the history, distribution and techniques of the craft. (These reviews cannot be purchased but may be borrowed through many public libraries.)

BATIK: WAX AND STARCH

The simplest definition of the Javanese word Batik, is that it is a resist technique for producing designs on fabric. The resist substances may be wax or starch. It is one of the most widely spread techniques of fabric decoration. Known in China in the seventh century A.D. and even earlier in India, batik techniques are also found in Japan, Central and South-Eastern Asia, Europe and in part of Africa. In Indonesia it was originally done by the women of the aristocracy and each piece took many months to complete. As the process became industrialized it was developed in 'colouring schools' or factories under the influence first of the Chinese and later on, the Dutch.

The actual processes were separated so that the preparation of the cloth, usually cotton or silk, was always performed by the men, and the wax painting done by the women except for the block printing which was usually carried out by Chinese or Arab men. Men also dyed the waxed cloths as well as preparing the dyestuffs and mordants used. Recently in Indonesia synthetic dyestuffs have almost completely superseded the natural dyestuffs once exclusively used.

Although most of the batik produced was for home consumption a lively export trade developed in the seventeenth century and this grew with the founding of various trading companies until Javanese batiks were found all over the civilized world. It is curious to note that whereas a batik with a crackle effect was not so acceptable to the Indonesians this particular quality has always been most prized in the West. Present-day craftsmen practising batik include Susan Bosence and Annette Kok of Dartington; Noel Dyrenforth; Michael O'Connell and E. V. Grueger.

If wax is the resist used, it is melted and applied hot to the fabric by brush, block (tjap) or written with a special tool called a 'tjanting'. When the wax is cold, the fabric is either painted all over or in part with dye or dipped in a dye bath. The wax 'resists' repel the dye, and the fabric protected by the wax remains the original colour of the material. As soon as the dye is dry the whole process can be repeated as often as required to obtain very complicated patterns.

Upon completion the resist is removed from the fabric either by heat (such as ironing), boiling or by the use of a solvent.

The resist can, of course, be cracked before dyeing to give a texture of fine lines.

Many other resists such as those made from starch pastes are used to obtain particular effects.

23 'Writing' the pattern with a tjanting full of hot wax.
Courtesy Department of Information, Djakarta, Indonesia.

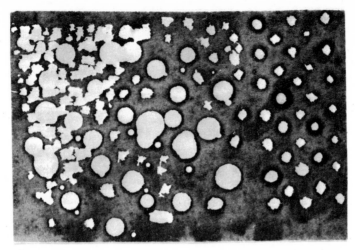

24 **A**

WAX RESISTS
SOME SIMPLE EXPERIMENTS
Waxing

1. (Figure 24.) First cover the table with a piece of American cloth (as it is called in Great Britain), plastic sheeting or a large opened up plastic bag. Place some flat pieces of scrap fabric (old handkerchief, pieces of sheet or pillowcase) on the plastic covering. Light a candle, hold it upright and close above the fabric. Tilt it and allow the drips of hot wax to fall on the fabric. See from how high you can safely drop the wax before it cools and sets *on* the fabric rather than *in* the fabric —where it must be if it is to resist the dye (A).

Turn the candle as it drips to obtain an even melting of the wax.

2. Place the paper or card shapes, tape, drawing pins, coins, strips of thin card or wood, etc., on the fabric in regular patterns. Then drop the wax from a candle as above. The shapes will mask out part of the fabric and give plain areas as against the areas patterned with drops of wax (B).

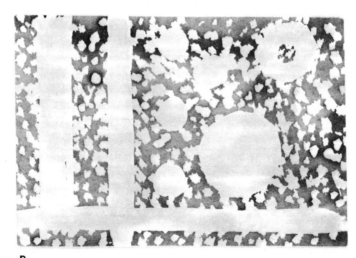

24 **B**

3. Pleat or fold the fabric so as to hide some parts under other parts or mask-off large areas or stripes with Sellotape, paper, card, polythene, etc., and proceed as before.

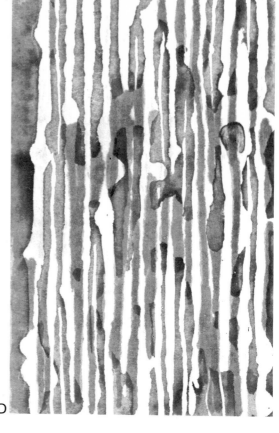

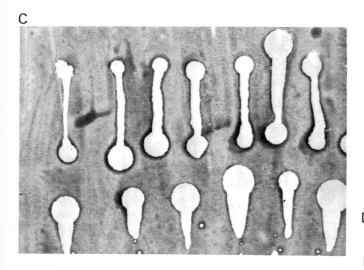

C

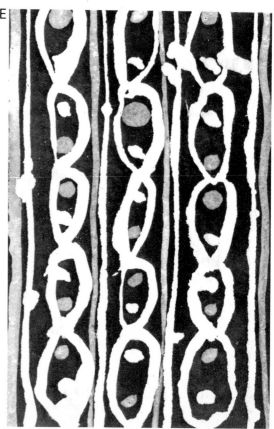

D

E

4. Pin a piece of cloth to a frame and prop the frame against a box and at an angle to the table top. As the candle drips on the cloth it will produce short runs rather than dots (C). Varying the angle produces different shapes. Following the trail of wax with the candle produces long runs (D). In (E) a second waxing and dyeing has been used.

5. (Figure 25.) Stand a lighted nightlight in a small tin or jar. Use a small brush or a sharpened wood stick to pick up the melted wax around the wick and apply as quickly as possible to the fabric.

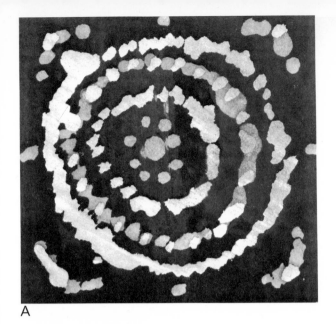

A

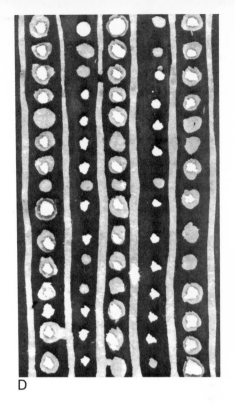

D

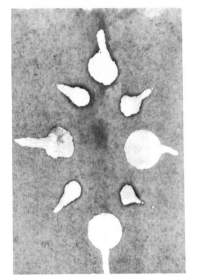

C

25 A—stick applied wax; B—dripped runs on a sloping fabric; C and E—drips from a nightlight held high; D—two-colour brush painted.

B

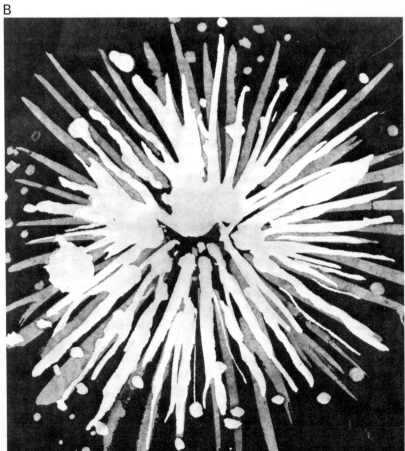

E

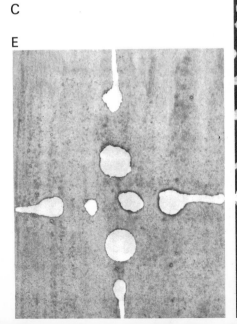

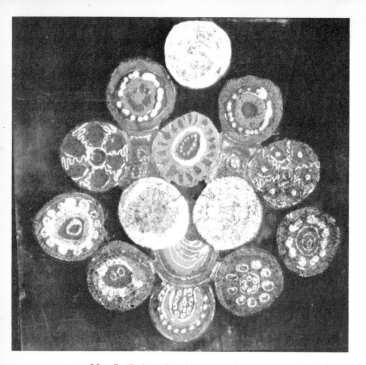

26 Batik hanging in tones of orange and red, 36 in. square—*Coventry College of Education.*

Dyeing

Dye by dipping the fabric in a dye bath. You may use any of the cold water dyes such as the Dylon cold dyes or the Procion M range of Reactive dyestuffs. Recipes are given with each tin of Dylon cold dye and a special leaflet is also obtainable. The Procion M dyes are prepared by the following simplified recipe. *Don't forget to use rubber gloves to protect your hands.* The quantities given will dye up to 2 yards depending on the thickness and type of fabric used.

1. Dissolve 2 level teaspoons of dye powder in half a teacup ($\frac{1}{4}$ pint) of warm water, not above 70°C.
2. Dissolve 1 level teaspoon of common (not iodized) salt in 1 pint of cold water.
3. Mix (1) and (2) in a large bowl. If necessary add more water to have sufficient liquid to cover the fabric to be dyed.

4. Wet the waxed fabric in lukewarm water and then immerse it in the liquid in the large bowl for five minutes and turn well, taking care not to remove flakes of wax.
5. Dissolve 3 level teaspoons of washing soda in a quarter of a teacup ($\frac{1}{8}$ pint) of warm water and add to the large bowl containing the fabric. Leave for a further fifteen minutes, turning as before.
6. Wearing rubber gloves gently squeeze surplus dye back into the large bowl.
7. Let the dyed fabric lie on several layers of newspaper on the floor for at least 2–3 hours or if possible overnight. A kettle boiling for a few moments in the same room will help fix the dye which, at this stage, develops more quickly in a warm, humid atmosphere. It may also be developed whilst still wet inside one or two plastic bags.
8. After this period, rinse well and wash thoroughly or boil for five minutes in a detergent ($\frac{1}{4}$ teaspoon–2 quarts of water) such as Stergene or Lissapol (UK), Duponol or Synthrapol (USA). Iron on the reverse on kitchen paper or scrap cloth. Repeat as necessary until all the wax is removed.
9. Reduce or increase the dye as the shade requires but do not shorten the times or reduce the salt or soda.
10. Clear up at once with cold water.
11. Dyestuff only dyes at full strength 2–3 hours after the soda has been added.
12. Avoid splashing the dye on clothes, floor, hands, etc. It stains and is almost impossible to remove from clothes.
13. At stage 8 the fabric may be dry-cleaned and not washed or ironed.

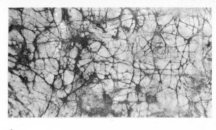

A

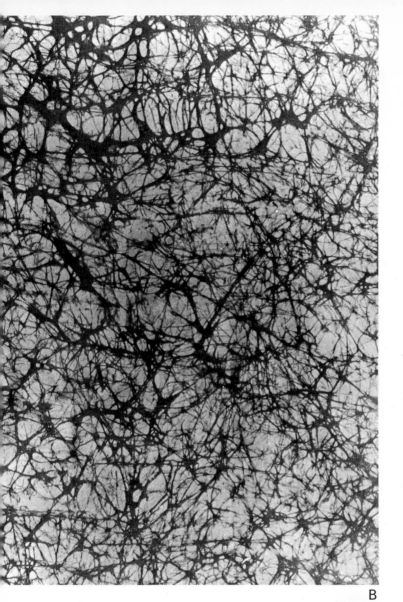

B

D

FURTHER WORK IN BATIK
Waxes (Figure 27)
The waxes used in Batik are of four types:
(1) This type is brittle and cracks easily, such as mineral or paraffin wax (one of the ingredients used to make candles).
(2) This type is sticky, such as rosin.
(3) This type is more pliable, such as beeswax.
(4) A cold type of wax is available in the U.S. called Dorland's Textile Wax. It is marketed by Durable Arts of San Rafael, California.

See page 36 for a description of the types of waxes that gave the different forms of 'crackle' shown here.

C

C

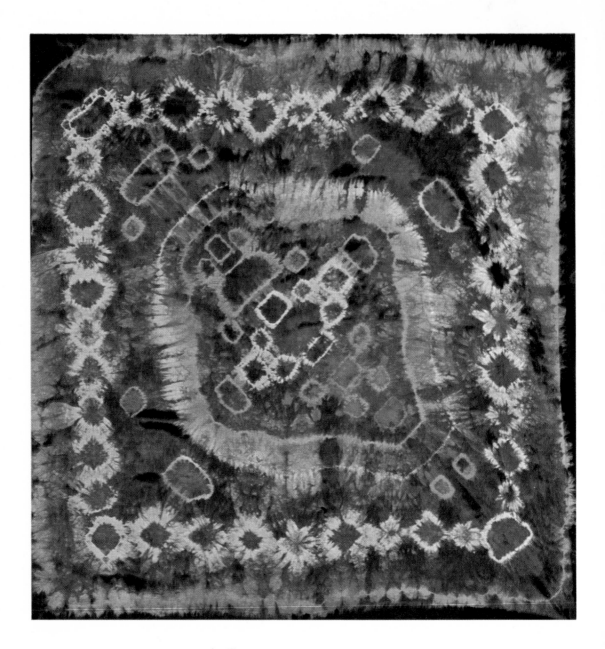

1 Tie dye on silk. *By Patricia Robinson.*

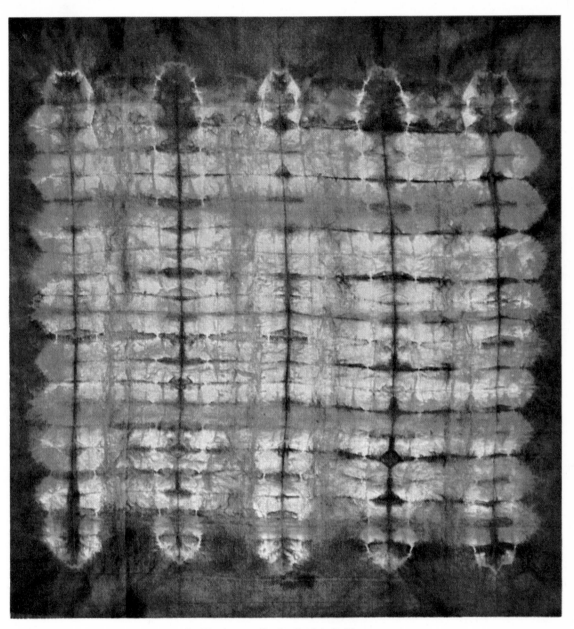

2   Tie dye on silk. *By Patricia Robinson.*

Most craftsmen develop their own mixture from these three waxes for the particular purpose it has to fulfil.

One of the delightful effects obtained is the hairline crackle produced by cracking the wax after it has been applied to the fabric (Figure 27A, page 33).

The more paraffin wax used in the mixture, the greater the areas of irregular crazing it is possible to obtain (B). But if too much paraffin wax is used and the wax is cracked it will tend to flake off and so leave patches of unprotected fabric (C).

A mixture of 1 part of beeswax–3 parts of paraffin wax is satisfactory; it is not advisable to reduce the paraffin wax content below one half of the whole if a crackle is required.

Where no crackle is required the wax may be pure beeswax plus a little rosin to make the wax adhere firmly to the fabric (D).

The wax is removed in a variety of ways;

1. By boiling off (*near* boiling in the case of silk and wool) in clean soft water. As long as no detergent or soap has been used, the wax may be skimmed off or allowed to set hard and used again even if it is coloured from the dyes used.

2. By ironing out with several layers of paper above and below the fabric. Most of the wax will be removed in this way although a number of changes of paper may be necessary. A final wash or washes in very hot water containing a little detergent will remove most of the remainder.

3. Some craftsmen employ baths of a cleaner such as Genklene (I.C.I.), benzene or petrol (both very inflammable). It should be noted that these last methods are *highly dangerous*, need plenty of space and air and are *not suitable for children.*

4. Most dry-cleaners will remove the wax at a moderate cost. This is one of the most satisfactory methods.

28 An example of a contemporary batik dress from Bombay. Notice the simple shape. *Courtesy UNEEK, Edgware Road, London.*

The wax is applied in several coats with different dyeings between each coat if more than one colour is required. It is most important that the wax is hot enough to penetrate the fabric upon application. If not, the back of a design must also be protected with more wax. If the wax, when applied, appears transparent and sinks into the material it is hot enough. If it turns opaque and lies on the surface it is too cool and will easily flake off the fabric.

If cost is the major consideration, as in school use, a most satisfactory 'crackle' mixture is 3 candles–1 disc of beeswax. Increase or decrease the candles for more or less crackle.

Waterless Wax Pots
29 Although the initial cost is somewhat higher than pots requiring water the waterless type are outstanding in the freedom they give the user. The thermostatic control keeps the wax at the right temperature, there is no container to boil dry and fire risks are eliminated. The electrical consumption is negligible.

Wax Kettles

It is not advisable to heat any kind of wax in a single saucepan. The best and safest way to keep it at an even temperature is to use an electric, waterless glue kettle with a screw thermostat control such as those supplied by Barlow-Whitney Ltd (see Batik Suppliers at end of chapter). Although more expensive initially these are safe in use and will last for many years without attention (Figure 29).

An ordinary glue pot with two containers, the outer, larger one for water and the smaller, inner one for wax, are also very suitable. They are obtainable from ironmongers and if heated by electricity can be controlled with a 'simmer' type of switch (Figure 30 A).

A double saucepan of the porridge type with water in the outer container is a cheap and efficient method of heating wax (B).

Whichever type of kettle is used it is essential that the inner container has a bar across the top on which to wipe off the surplus wax or on which to rest the brush or tjanting. This prevents the wax running down the outside of the kettle.

In all cases where the wax is heated over water it is important to:
(1) frequently check the water level and top up as required,
(2) avoid dropping water in the hot wax, and
(3) not allow the wax to actually boil.

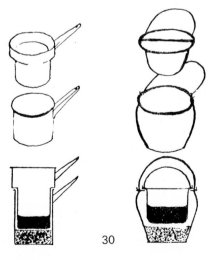

30

A   B

3 Batik hanging employing Procion M dyes. *Ann Milsum, Coventry College of Education.*

Tools

A brush, pointed wooden stick or spoon can be used to apply the wax. The most common tools are brushes of various widths. One can be trimmed to a wedge shape as in Figure 31. This form allows fine lines or large areas to be waxed with the same brush. To cut a wedge shape, first fill the brush with hot wax. If the brush splays outwards gently press against the side of the inner wax container to release air and moisture trapped inside the brush. Allow the wax brush to cool and then cut the bristles diagonally with scissors or a sharp knife.

32 B

31

32 A

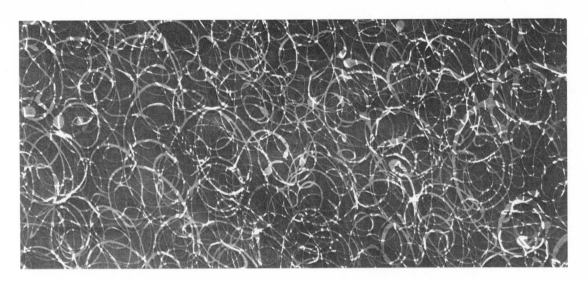

33 Tjanting drawn patterns then dyed light green and further tjanting patterning before dyeing in deep blue—*Patricia Robinson.*

The 'tjanting' is a traditional Javanese wax trailer (Figure 32A), modern versions of which may still be purchased from several suppliers (32B). As will be seen it consists of a metal cup and spout fastened to a wooden handle. The tjanting cup is warmed in the hot wax, half-filled, tipped slightly backwards to stop dripping from the spout, then taken to the fabric. The spout end is placed on the fabric and the tjanting tipped slightly forward to allow the hot wax to flow out of the spout. By moving and tipping, a most attractive pattern of dots and lines may be built up. As the wax cools in the spout, a dip into the hot wax container will keep it flowing. To avoid unwanted spots of wax on the fabric, carry the brush or tjanting spout over a piece of rag held in the other hand.

Electrically heated tjantings with a thermostatic control are often used by craftsmen.

Printing sticks or stamps may be made from strips of cloth wrapped around square or round wood dowelling (Figure 34 A). Metal stamps (such as are used in bookbinding decoration, (B), small metal lids and caps attached to a wood stick as handle (C), pieces of hollow brass tube, washers, nuts, etc., stuck to a wood stick or rolls of corrugated paper (D) will all retain hot wax and mark off on to the fabric.

34

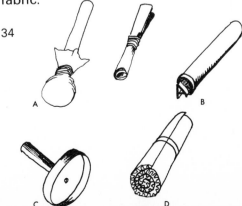

Waxing Frames (Figure 35)

If the fabric is waxed on top of a plastic bag or American cloth is stretched over

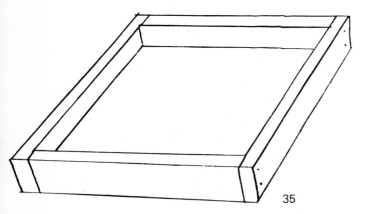

35

the table it will often happen that very hot wax goes through the fabric and sticks it to the plastic covering. When pulled off much wax is left on the plastic and parts of the back of the fabric will be uncovered. To avoid this, one can clip or pin the fabric to some type of frame. An old picture frame, a silk screen frame, a box lid will all serve to hold the fabric away from the table top. This will allow the hot wax to penetrate and saturate the fabric on both sides. When applied to the fabric the wax must be translucent in appearance and penetrate around the fibres. As has been stressed before, it should not merely be on the surface or it will not protect the fibres from the dye.

Marking out the Fabric (Figure 36)

Lines and dots marked out in pencil or chalk often cannot be removed as they are trapped indelibly by the dye or wax. Where a pencil is used it should be a soft one and used very faintly and in dots rather than lines. Designs can be drawn with a sharpened candle, white wax pencil or crayon. Guide lines may be pressed with a warm iron into the folded material before it is opened out and stretched over a frame.

In many ways the most satisfactory method of marking out is to use lines of thread stretched across the fabric and fastened to the frame edge (A).

For straight lines of wax a strip or batten of wood may be laid across the fabric and frame to act as a guide rail. It will keep the hand and brush along a reasonably straight line (B).

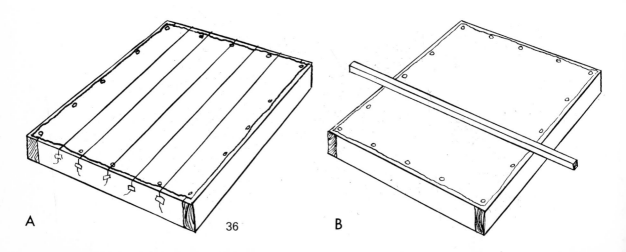

A

36

B

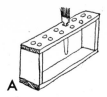

37   A—a simply made brush block; B—a kitchen table or desk covered with padding and plastic sheet to make a work place. Keep wax near to fabric with one rack for wax brushes and one for dye brushes.

38   Part of a nineteenth-century Javanese batik showing the redyeing of indigo with soga brown after rewaxing. *Collection James Howard Esq.*

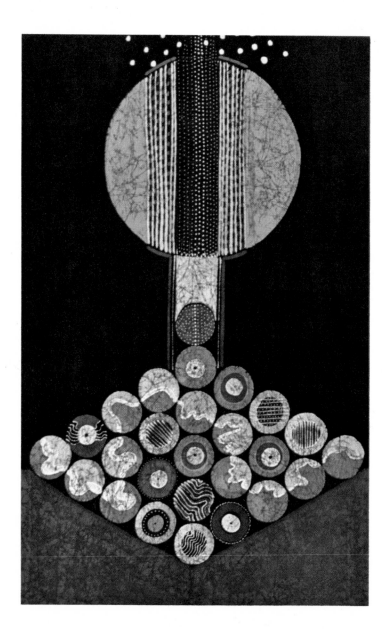

4   A Batik hanging by Noel Dyrenforth. Born in London in 1936, he studied
painting and drawing, worked in fabric design, printing and advertising
until 1962 when he commenced Batik. This example is one of a series of
twelve on 'Spring', and is executed with Procion M dyes. He now lives and
works in London.

5   Another Batik hanging by Noel Dyrenforth employing Procion dyes.

39 Candle waxed handkerchief in two colours by a primary school pupil.

It may be necessary to apply dye to some parts of the fabric which have already been waxed. Unless this wax has been completely removed, traces of it left on the fabric will resist further dyeing. In most cases complete stripping of wax on the whole of the fabric will be necessary. It is obvious that it is best to plan the wax/dye/wax/dye, etc. sequence to avoid the removal of wax in order to redye.

40 A wax painted and dyed Easter egg from Bohemia. *Courtesy CIBA Review.*

Dyes

The cold water dyes such as Dylon cold (UK) and RIT or Tintex (USA) or the Procion M range already mentioned are the most suitable for Batik. It is also possible to use Polyprint or other Pigment dyes but with these dyestuffs the wax must be removed by *dry* ironing which also fixes the Polyprint at the same time. The Polyprint must be allowed to dry before ironing and it is ironed with the Polyprinted side to the newspaper and away from the iron.

Similarly, quite a high degree of fixation can be obtained from most other dyestuffs such as Acid, Direct, Cibacron, Procion H, etc. dyes, but some experimenting is necessary. The dye is mixed to the appropriate recipe for Screen Printing and, when dry, ironed to fix with a *steam* iron. The difficulty is that the iron must be of a temperature to suit the fabric that has been printed and must remain in total for about three minutes on any one part if the dye is to be fully fixed.

GENERAL NOTES

1. Allow sufficient margins to fabrics before you apply your design. You will then be able to stretch, fringe, hem or frame your work without losing parts of the design.
2. It is, of course, possible to use fabrics with self patterns, stripes, spots and to produce further patterns on top of these with batik.

FURTHER EXPERIMENTS

1. Using a brush or tjanting and a batten to guide the hand, draw regular parallel stripes of wax along the fabric. When the wax is dry and cold, crack across the stripes to give a fine crackle. Paint a light or medium-coloured dye over the fabric and work into the crackle. Blot off any surplus dye with clean newspaper. This is often necessary if the dye creeps under the wax where it is not required.

When the dye is dry, rewax and re-crack the stripes and insert a row of dots down the unwaxed stripes. Re-dye in a slightly deeper or contrasting colour. Allow the dye to fix and remove as before.

2. Use threads to divide the fabric into small squares, oblongs or diamond shapes. With a brush or tjanting draw small units in wax (such as snow crystals, Chinese letters, Egyptian hieroglyphics) in each shape. When the wax is dry, paint dye all over the fabric. Dry and paint the wax over the fabric, carefully crackle all the waxed fabric and paint a second dye into the crackle lines, blotting as necessary. Allow the dye to fix and remove as before.

3. It is possible to change the bright Procion M colours to various rich dark brown shades by, either painting over the dyed but unfixed fabric with, or immersing it in, a bath consisting of 1 part Brentamine Fast Black K Salt (UK), Fast Black K Salt (USA)–50 parts of water. This is done *before* the Procion M dye has been fixed.

The colour change is almost instantaneous and, when evenly developed throughout, wash as before.

The fabric may be rewaxed after any dyeing and before the Brentamine is applied. Different Procion M dyes change to various shades of brown, e.g. Procion Brilliant Red M-2BS plus Brentamine Fast Black K Salt gives reddish brown;

41 'Pop group' batik hanging in Procion M dyes by *Barbara Wolstenholme—Coventry College of Education.*

Procion Yellow M-RS, however, gives yellowish brown and Procion Blue M-3GS gives chocolate brown.

4. Wax lines may be applied as enclosing barriers to contain different colours of dye or with gateways to allow the dye to flow out and spread in fanlike shapes into the unwaxed material. Again when dry, fresh waxing and dyeing may be employed as before.

5. Where large areas of plain fabric are to be resisted and left the original colour, a piece of greaseproof paper may be sello-taped to the fabric or a piece of cardboard, metal, plastic or wood cut out and fixed with double-sided sellotape in order to save the use of wax when covering large areas.

STARCH RESISTS
SOME SIMPLE EXPERIMENTS
Basic method using Polyprint (or other Pigment dyestuffs).

NOTE: Separate brushes should be used for paste and Polyprint.

1. Mix plain flour with water to the consistency of thick batter. Vary according to the type of 'crackle' required—thick paste gives a larger crackle, thinner paste gives a finer crackle.

2. Paint the paste onto the fabric and wash out the brush in cold water *immediately* after use.

3. *Dry thoroughly*—the material will then be puckered.

4. Pull the fabric so that the flour paste cracks.

5. Mix Polyprint (1 part Polyprint colour– 9 parts of Polyprint binder).

6. Paint Polyprint over the paste. (Look on the reverse of the fabric to check the crackle effect) and wash out the brush in cold water *immediately* after use.

7. Dry thoroughly.

8. Fix Polyprint by placing the fabric, paste side down on a pad of several sheets of newspaper. Cover with one sheet of newspaper and iron for three minutes at appropriate heat for the fabric used. Keep the iron moving. It is essential with a large piece of fabric that each part is ironed for at least three minutes.

9. Rinse in cold water.

10. Place on newspaper, scrape off the paste with the back of an old knife or bone folder or old ruler and throw the paste away in newspaper.

11. Rinse the fabric thoroughly and iron on the reverse side on top of paper.

12. Clear up. Use cold water to wash off any splashes of Polyprint or paste. Put any mixed Polyprint in a screw-topped jar, label 'Mixed Polyprint' and return to a cool store cupboard for future use.

42   Three types of starch resist crackle Top-thick paste; middle-medium paste; lower-thin paste.

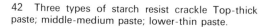

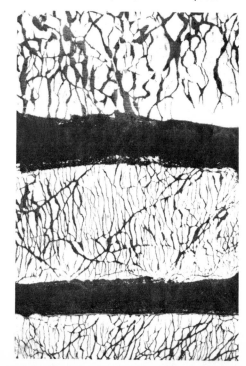

FURTHER EXPERIMENTS

1. This flour paste 'resist' may also be used with Procion M dyestuffs. Use the recipe already given in wax resist (on page 32) but thicken with Manutex RS (page 143). Proceed as above to stage 7 when the dye is fixed by leaving the fabric in the room overnight. Then follow from stage 9 but do not save the mixed Procion M dye.

2. Procion H, Cibacron and other Reactive dyestuffs thickened with Manutex may also be used and reasonable fixation can be achieved by steam ironing when the dye is dry especially if the catalyst recipe is used (see page 138).

3. Considerable experimenting may be carried out with different pastes for different purposes. A starch paste may be made from equal parts, say 1 level teaspoon of starch, ground rice and plain flour in 1 pint of water. Mix and cook as with thin custard and paint on the fabric whilst still hot. Leave to set hard before using dyes with a brush or block. After fixing the dye, remove by several washings (or boilings if the dye permits this).

Other pastes such as cold water paste, Polycell, PVC paste, gum and plain flour or any adhesive that is not or does not become completely waterproof when dry are also possible resists.

Pastes can be applied through a stencil, by piping through an icing syringe, slip trailer or forcing bag. It can also be printed from a pad with potatoes, scraps, lino blocks, etc. To avoid undue drying out, a few drops of glycerine should be added to the paste.

43 An example of a starch resist using soledon dyes in brown and blue with a second starching on the first dyeing. Original in Victoria and Albert Museum. *Courtesy Susan Bosence, Dartington.*

SUPPLIERS OF BATIK MATERIALS

In addition to the firms mentioned in the general list of suppliers the following are particularly recommended for Batik supplies. (Fabrics—see page 151; Dyes see page 123.)

Great Britain

Candlemakers Supplies—101 Moore Park Road, London S.W.6 for all types of waxes, Procion M, Acid, Direct and Mordant dyes and chemicals.

Dryad Handicrafts—Northgates Leicester for tjantings, fabrics and wax.

D. Mackay—85 East Road, Cambridge for tjantings.

Prices candles (from Hardware & Timothy Whites Stores).

Boots the Chemists for Paraffin Wax, Beeswax.

Barlow-Whitney Ltd—Sales Division, Coombe Road, Neasden, London N.10 for Waterless Glue Kettle.

Polyprint—Polyprint, 815 Lisburn Road, Belfast, BT9 7GX, N. Ireland.

Dylon Cold Water Dyes—chemists, Hardware and multiple stores (request a leaflet on how to use) or from

Procion M Dyes—Mayborn Products Ltd, Dylon Works, Sydenham, London S.E.26 (also Lissapol D, Brentamine Fast Salts, Manutex & Chemicals).

Sweden

Beckers—Sveavägen 42, Stockholm, for wax, dyes etc.

USA

Aquaprint—Interchem, New Jersey.

Art & Crafts Materials Corporation—321 Park Avenue, Maryland, Baltimore 1.

Craft Tools Inc.—396 Broadway, New York 13, N.Y.

Durable Arts—P.O. Box 2413, San Rafael, California, for Dorland's cold textile wax and versatex water soluble permanent textile colours.

Procion M Dyes—Arnold Hoffman & Co., Inc., 55 Canal Street, Providence, Rhode Island.

Prang Aqua Pigment Textile Colours and Acco-Lite colors—The American Crayon Company, Sandusky, Ohio.

Aiko's Art Materials Import—714 N. Wabash Avenue, Chicago, Ill.

Bengen Arts & Crafts—Shetland Industrial Park, Salem, Mass.

Dick Blick—P.O. Box 1267, Galesburg, Ill.

CCM Arts & Crafts, Inc.—9520, Baltimore Avenue, College Park, Md.

Creative Hands Co. Inc.—4146 Library Road, Pittsburgh, Pa.

Kilns Inc.—225 Mamaroneck Avenue, Mamaroneck, N.Y.

Triarco Arts & Crafts—P.O. Box 106 Northfields, Ill.

Waldcroft—P.O. Box 8202, Lexington, Ky.

Yasutomo & Co.—24 California Street, San Francisco, California.

FURTHER SOURCES FOR MORE ADVANCED BATIK

Apart from the books mentioned in the General Bibliography the following are also recommended:

Batik by Ila Keller, Prentice Hall, London, 1967.

Useful well-arranged information with step-by-step details and well-chosen illustrations.

Batik—Art and Craft by Nik Krevitsky, Reinhold, N.Y., 1964.

A practical, well-illustrated book covering most aspects of the craft. These two recent books are especially recommended.

The Book of Batik by Ernst Muehling, Mills and Boon, London, 1967.

Introducing Batik by Evelyn Samuel, Batsford, London, 1968.

Batik—Burns and Oates, London, 1969.

The following publications are useful for historical details, illustrations and dye recipes up to date of publication.

Batik by Alfred Steinmann, F. Lewis, Leigh on Sea, 1958.

Decorative Art in Indonesian Textiles by Laurens Langewis and Frits Wagner, F. Lewis, Leigh on Sea, 1964.

CIBA Review No. 58 Batiks, The Editors, Ciba Review, Basle, Switzerland.

A standard monograph upon the history, distribution and techniques of the craft. (These reviews cannot be purchased but may be borrowed through many public libraries.)

Batik and other pattern dyeing by W. D. and I. S. Baker, Atkinson, Mentzer & Co., Chicago, 1920.

Good, historical background, useful dyeing information with older forms of dyes and design.

Batiks and how to make them by P. Mijer, Dodd Mead & Co., N.Y., 1924.

Very good historical account of Java, Dutch and USA with older forms of dyes and designs.

First lessons in Batik by G. C. Lewis, Dryad Press, Leicester, 1921.

Good illustrations to date of publication.

Batik by J. Irwin and V. Murphy, V. & A., H.M.S.O., 1969.

Maintains the usual high standard of V. & A. publications.

PAD PRINTING WITH VEGETABLES AND SCRAPS

The use of a stamp as a method of decoration goes back to early times. Carved wooden or bone stamps were used as seals in ancient Babylon to be impressed on clay tablets, the writing material of the times. They`were used as coloured ink stamps in China, and as a means of decorating pottery in many parts of the world. In Polynesia and parts of Africa, the built-up stamp is still used in the manufacture of decorated Tapa or Bark cloth, as well as the gourd stamp which is carved into simple pattern units and printed upon bark or leaf cloth such as the Adinkira cloths of West Africa.

Examples of early hand stamped textiles dating from before the seventh century A.D. have not yet come to light. However stamps, in other words, very small wooden cylinders with engraved patterns, and small pieces of printed cotton cloth have been found in the sands of North Africa, showing stylized leaf patterns. It has been thought that the art of stamping came to Byzantium from Persia. Stamps were also used to produce wax resist patterns in Batik work.

The earliest dyestuffs used in pad printing were, probably insoluble pigments such as soot, ruddle (red-ochre) and other earths, ground in oil.

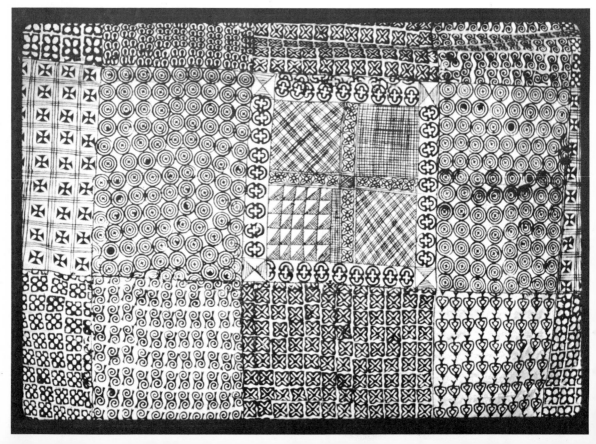

44A   Left—Adinkira cloth. This is an example of printing in a tar-like ink from gourd stamps by the Ashanti tribe, near Kumasi, Ghana. *Courtesy of the Trustees of the British Museum (Ethnographical Department).*

44B   Above—a painted bark-fibre cloth from the Fiji Islands. Made by pounding tree bark containing soot and tree-gums. *Courtesy Museum of Applied Arts, Zurich and CIBA Review.*

As techniques improved, different geographical areas became noted for specialist development of particular forms of block printing. In the early Middle Ages, simple wood stamps flourished in parts of Germany, and large blocks were used in other parts of Europe by the fifteenth century. In the main, these printed textiles were for ecclesiastical purposes but gradually the process spread to the printing of patterned fabrics for clothing and furnishing with the development of large wood engravings and metal plates.

In the Near East, the manufacture of 'pin' and 'metal strip' blocks had developed into a most intricate and skilful craft. These were printed from a pad suspended in a dye bath. So too were the elaborate blocks prepared in Europe to celebrate special events such as the defeat of Napoleon. Eventually the engraved block became a plate fitted around a roller and the dye pad turned into another felt covered feed roller soaked in dye. This rotated against the engraved roller, covering it with an even coating of dye to print the pattern off onto the cloth as the rollers of this outsize 'mangle' turned at high speed.

Today Block printing is only practised by hand craftsmen. Other forms of Pad printing using potato, swede, carrot, cabbage, sprouts and other vegetables, scrap blocks, embossed papers, bottle tops, corrugated cardboard and the like are used extensively in school work.

45   A Paisley block built up of copper pins and metal strips inserted into a wood block. Note the guiding pins near the corners. A separate block was necessary for each colour and great skill was required to keep a perfect register between block and block. Very complicated design might require more than 100 impressions per yard. The lead mallet was used to tap the back to obtain even prints. *Courtesy Liberty of London.*

BASIC EQUIPMENT FOR PAD PRINTING

1. Cover the table with a piece of plastic sheeting, American cloth or a large, opened-out plastic bag.

2. For a printing pad, use a piece of *thin* plastic foam sheet, felt or any absorbent fabric (even a wad of newspaper, paper handkerchiefs or soft toilet paper covered with a piece of buttermuslin or bandage) large enough to take the vegetable, block, etc. to be used. Place this on a small piece of plastic, a tin lid or tile.

3. For trial prints you will require kitchen or newsprint paper. Old newspaper without too many pictures may be used. For *good* prints, any fabric with a fairly smooth, absorbent surface is suitable.

4. Most dyestuffs may be used, but for simple experimental work, we thoroughly recommend any of the very wide range of Lawrence's fabric inks mixed with Lawrence's thinning oil. As an alternative, we suggest a Pigment dyestuff such as Polyprint or Printex or any household oil paint thinned with turpentine.

If Lawrence's fabric inks are used, prepare as follows:

Squeeze a 2 in. length of the ink into a small screw-topped jar and stir in 2 level dessertspoonsful of Lawrence's thinning oil to give the consistency of thin cream. *Note* (a) Pale colours made with the addition of white have a chalkier quality than those to which Lawrence's reducing medium has been added.

(b) When mixing a pale colour, always mix white or lightest colour first, adding deeper tones last. It only requires a small amount of black to turn several times the same quantity of white into dark grey.

(c) Allow prints to dry overnight; although some will dry in 1–2 hours others —particularly black—may take up to 36 hours.

(d) Fabrics may be used when the ink is completely dry. They may be washed as necessary, in soap or mild detergent, rinsed and ironed on the reverse side when ready. The first wash usually improves the appearance and 'feel' of the printed fabric.

46 **A**

If Polyprint (GB), Printex (GB), Aquaprint (USA) or Prang (USA) dyestuff is used, follow the usual mixing method of 1 part Polyprint–9 parts of binder, or as the makers specify and, *when the print is dry*, fix by ironing on the back of the fabric for a few moments with a warm iron.

Avoid prolonged boiling or excessive rubbing whilst washing.

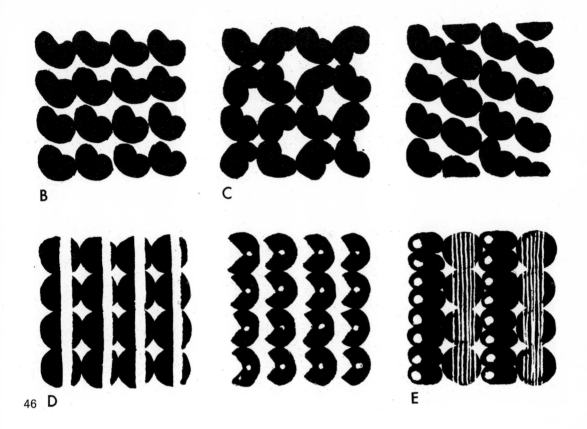

B C

46 D E

SOME SIMPLE EXPERIMENTS
WITH VEGETABLES ON PAPER

1. (Figure 46.) Prepare the printing pad.
(A) Halve a large potato with a large knife to keep a flat printing surface and blot on the scrap paper.
(B) Press the cut surface of one half of the potato onto the pad several times to 'charge' it properly, and then firmly press it onto the newspaper. Re-charge it, and print again, then repeat until you have a large block of prints (say 5 by 5 in. or 6 by 6 in.), all the same way up, all touching at the top and sides.

(C) Always re-charge before printing and add more dye to the pad as is necessary.

Experiment with different ways of placing the potato prints on the newspaper.
(D) Cut or tear strips of paper, place on the printing paper and print across these.
(E) Place other shapes between the potato and its print such as paper stars, circles, triangles or cut/torn paper shapes or a length of tape, slub threads, lace, etc.

As the potato picks up the small pieces these must be peeled off and replaced in the next printing position before re-charging the potato from the pad. Strips and lengths may be fastened down with sellotape to hold them in position.

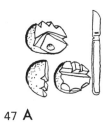

47 A

2. (Figure 47.) Experiment with the potato, cut it oblong or square or triangular by cutting off complete sides, and then cut the patterns with a penknife (A).

Try printing with an unpatterned surface in a block, then patterning the potato and printing on top of the original flat print (B).

To keep printing regular, follow a newspaper column of type (C).

3. Invent new ways of arranging your potato pattern (D). Avoid too complicated repeats, use strips of paper to mark unprinted spaces between strips of pattern, or lines of cotton stuck down with gumstrip or sellotape at each end (E).

4. (Figure 48.) Using kitchen or newsprint paper on which to work, print a table mat (A). Experiment with a simply cut potato as a first colour and the same potato with more cutting for a second colour (B). Use pieces of newspaper as masks to mitre corners (C) or centre space (D).

5. The above ideas may be used to produce patterned papers for bookcraft.

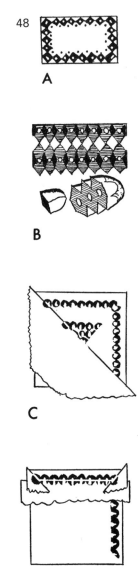

48

A

B

C

D

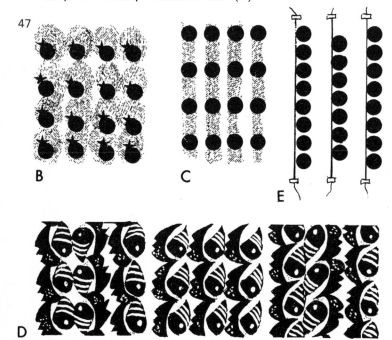

47

B

C

E

D

6   Block-printed silk scarf. *Designed by Margaret Holgate, printed by Patricia Robinson.*

49

6. (Figure 49.) Other vegetables will give different qualities of print, particularly carrots, the closer texture of which allows much finer cutting, the same is true of swedes, turnips, sugar beet, etc.

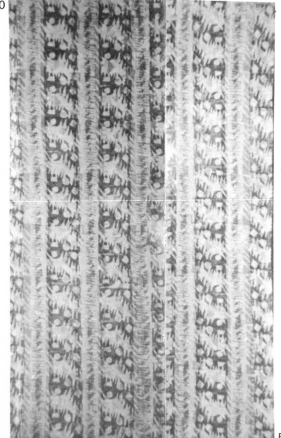

50

SOME SIMPLE EXPERIMENTS WITH VEGETABLES ON FABRIC

1. Table mats, glass mats, scarves, ties, pin cushions, aprons, cushion covers and similar articles as well as lengths of fabric, bedspreads, tablecloths and matching napkins may all be printed with vegetables.

It is often best to start by cutting out with pinking shears a table mat from a piece of old household linen and then printing upon it without too much preliminary planning apart from mitring the corners if required.

50 Work by primary school children. A—lengths of potato cut printed lengths in several colours using Lawrence's ink thinned as described in the text. B—Apron printed with potato cuts and sponge in Polyprint from a pad. C—Tie dyed handkerchief overprinted with potato and matchstick prints in thinned inks. D—table mats by 6-year-olds using potato cuts and thinned inks.

50 A

50

B

C

D

58

7   Lino block printed table mats in Lawrence's inks. *Designed by 1st-year students, Coventry College of Education.*

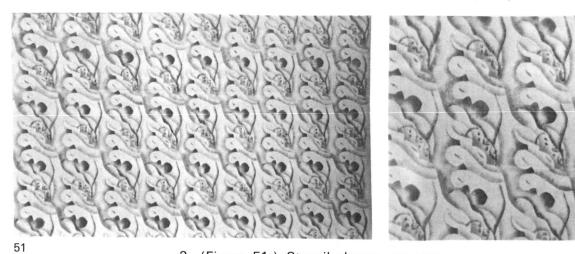

51

2. (Figure 51.) Stencil shapes are very useful for printing controlled patterned and unpatterned areas.

8 Screen-printed hanging in Cibacron (catalyst method) dyes. *Kay Coulson, Coventry College of Education.*

52

3. (Figure 52.) Brussels sprouts and tightly packed cabbages cut in half and printed in the same way give useful background textures and individual tree-like units.

4. (Figure 53.) Pads may be charged in two or more colours at once, and so give various colours with only one printing. *Care* must be taken to place the potato back on the same place on the pad or the colours will merge and may become muddy.

53

54   A splatter pattern obtained by dipping a toothbrush into dye and scraping the surface with a piece of card to splash dots of dye on a piece of fabric.

55

OTHER PRINT FORMS

1. (Figure 55.) Natural prints may be made from leaves with well-defined outlines such as fern (particularly attractive), ash, hawthorn, oak, plane, horse chestnut, poplar, sycamore, etc. or those with strongly marked veins, such as chestnut, ivy, laurel, plane, white beam, etc. Feathers of all types, especially those with unusual shapes or edges, dried flowers, leaf stems, sections of cones, nut shells such as walnuts, coconuts, etc. Most of these may be printed in three ways.

(a) Rest the leaf or leaves, etc., onto the printing pad, place a piece of clean newspaper on top, press gently, remove the newspaper, place the leaves in correct position on the fabric with a clean piece of newspaper on top, and press gently. When the newspaper and leaf are removed, a print will remain on the fabric.

By this method, and by using a number of differently coloured pads, it is possible to print several colours or a complete design all at the same time.

(b) The piece of newspaper first used can also be printed by merely pressing it on the fabric where it will give a mottled background texture and a white shape. Other methods may then be printed on top.

(c) The leaf may be glued to a piece of cardboard, hardboard or plywood and printed off, the background or the piece of board will also print.

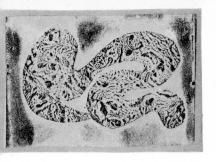

56 A piece of embossed wallpaper mounted on a piece of hardboard and printed from a pad.

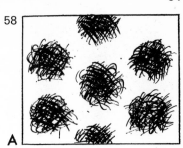

A

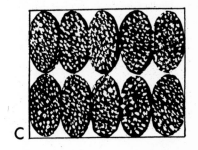

B

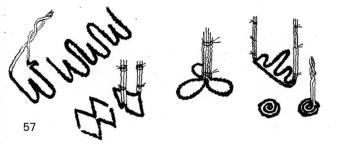

57

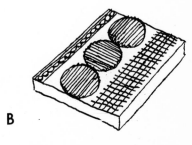

C

2. (Figure 57.) Pipe cleaners and heavy covered wire may be bent into shapes with the ends standing up to form a handle. Hold the 'handles' to press the shape on the pad and then on the fabric. Tie with thread, or twist several pipe cleaners together to make more complicated units.

3. (Figure 58.) Other materials such as packing straw and shavings of all types, or old rag bunched together and held in the hand (A); coarse canvas, rug canvas, corrugated paper, embossed wallpapers, etc., which may be cut into shapes and mounted on a block (B); and natural sponges, loofahs, synthetic sponges, latex and plastic foam, carpet underlay, polystyrene packing may be used directly from a printing pad (C).

D

4. Again, torn or cut out paper shapes may be placed on the fabric *before* printing in order to leave white shapes against an overall background texture (D and E).

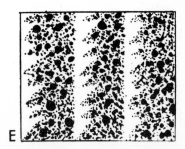

E

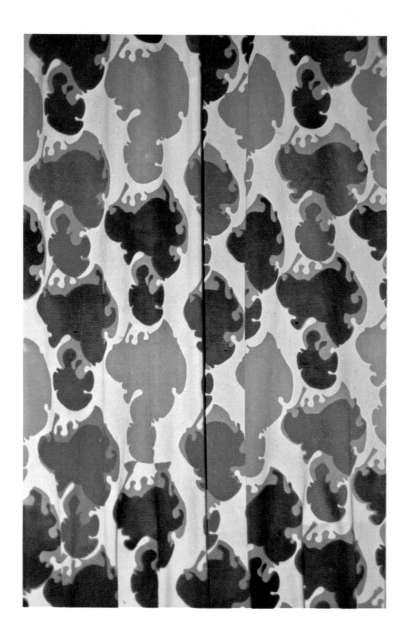

9 Screen-printed length in Cibacron colours on cotton satin. *Kay Coulson, Coventry College of Education.*

10   Screen-printed design. *Barbara Wolstenholme, Coventry College of Education.*

5. (Figure 59.) Scrap prints from a collection of bottle tops, washers, scent and other small or unusually shaped bottles, jars, tins, plastic containers, lids, different sizes of sections of cardboard rolls cut to give ovals as well as circles, scraps of wood, dowelling, match and other small boxes. Merely press these on the pad and they will print. Various shapes may be combined to form new shapes and patterns. Several colours will build up to give a rich, all over effect. They are particularly attractive when printed in stripes.

59 Actual prints from a variety of container tops and other scrap materials.

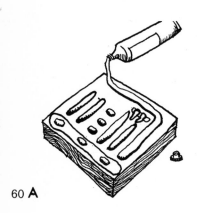

B

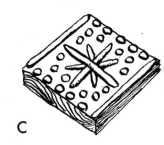

60 **A**

C

6. (Figure 60.) Drip prints are produced by dripping and trailing glues upon a small piece of board. Most of the common glues available in handyman stores are suitable. Ones that are especially good, since they dry quickly and without undue shrinking are Bateman's Household Adhesive, Evostik 528, Weldite and Bostik 3. Other possibilities open to experiment are old *thick* paint (cellulose, enamel, varnish, Japlac and Chinese lacquers: any paint will thicken up if left for a while without a lid, and the sediment used rather than the solvent). Fine sawdust can be mixed with the paint, as well as plastic wood or filling if required to give additional textures.

The block may be a piece of tough cardboard or a block of wood, blockboard or thick ply scraps preferably square, 4 by 4 in. being a good size for first experiments.

Without any preliminary planning or drawing, squeeze out the glue from the tube, or drip from a stick, directly onto the backing board (A). Build up a pattern and leave to set hard, then print from a pad (B). The background of the board will print as well as the drips. To prevent the edges of the block printing, place a run of glue near the edge (C).

Patterns may be built up with further drips upon, across or between the original drips. The height of the built up portions governs the areas of white appearing in the finished print.

This method is not so liable to chance as first appears, quite definite and planned patterns can be developed, as well as the typical blob shapes.

Larger blocks can be used to produce a handkerchief from one print, or a scarf from four prints.

Experiments are essential if lively and original work of any kind is to be produced in fabric printing. These simple drip blocks provide a cheap preliminary introduction to lino and wood blocks.

Developments include the printing of a block in one pale colour, for example grey, and overprinting the same block, but turned upside down, in black (D).

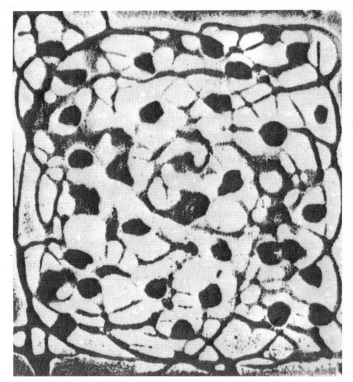

61

60 D

Misprinting, where an overprint is deliberately placed a little to one side, or is turned round a few degrees, or where prints are staggered, inverted in rows, printed draughtsboard pattern or tête beche, are all fruitful ideas (Figure 61).

Beads, buttons, peas, lentils, matches, string, rug wool, etc., may all be pressed into the glue while it is still 'tacky' to provide a sharp, contrasting shape to the softer, more rounded drip patterns. The following experiments are developments of this last technique.

E

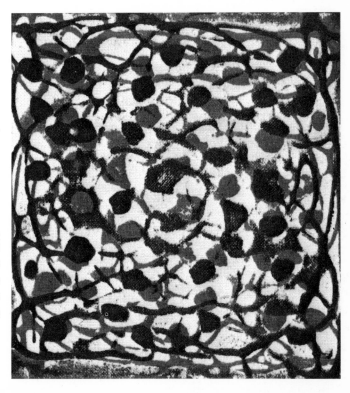

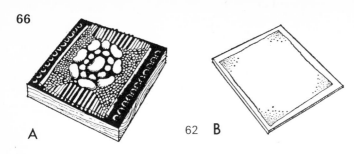

A   62 **B**

63

FURTHER EXPERIMENTS

1. (Figure 62.) Dried vegetables and cereal shapes, such as butter and haricot beans, split peas, pearl barley, macaroni, spaghetti (any shapes or length), may all be glued to a backing. When dry, the block will print if it has been prepared in the following manner:

Place a thick blob of glue such as Evo-stik 528, Bostik 1 or 3 in the centre of the backing and place the flat side of, for example, a butter bean in the blob. Make a pattern by glueing other dried cereals around this bean. Obtain a good variety by concentrating large cereals in one place and using smaller grains for the background textures (A).

After the glue has set, brush or spray a coat of varnish (Valspar or Permoglaze exterior clear varnish are quick drying) over the whole of the cereals and background of the printing side of the block and leave to dry. Next, *gently* rub the block, face downwards onto a sheet of fine sandpaper to give a slight tooth to the raised parts of the design (B). Blow away any dust from block, and print from the pad as before.

2. (Figure 63.) String prints that incorporate all kinds of smooth and hairy strings, picture, blind and sash cords, thin ropes, cloth-covered electric flex or cable, pipe cleaners, woven cotton and silk cords and other similar materials of medium thickness. Spread the glue in a thick layer over the side of the backing block, allow to become tacky and arrange the string and other materials in shapes and patterns. If necessary, tack, pin or staple to hold down. Allow to dry, then print from a pad. Different sizes of string on the same block give an interesting variety of print. Pack the strings closely together and allow the background to print as well.

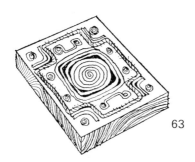

63

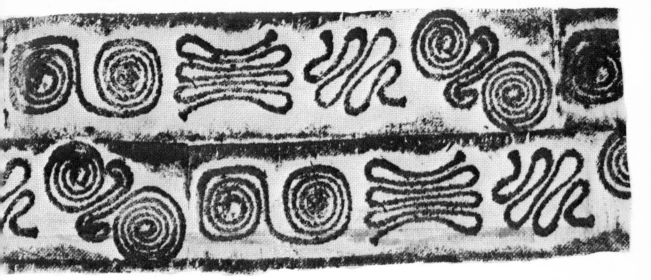

3. (Figure 64.) Nail prints are built up from a variety of nails driven into $\frac{3}{4}$ in. or 1 in. blockboard backing. (Still used extensively in the Far East, this form of block is easy to make and can be exceedingly varied in design.) We have found it possible to collect over 100, 1 in. nails and pins and all with different-sized or shaped heads from round, square or oblong monsters over $\frac{1}{2}$ in. across the top to the finest oval or round heads. Drive them into a 1-in. softwood block until about $\frac{5}{8}$ in. is protruding. As long as all the heads are level the block will print.

Other possibilities include the use of corrugated 'dogs' driven into a block or nuts, washers, sections of metal pipe or strip, sections of metal extrusions all cut to the same length and embedded in a layer of waterproof glue spread on top of the block.

64 An Indian print from a block made from nails and metal strips driven in to a piece of hard wood and printed from a pad.

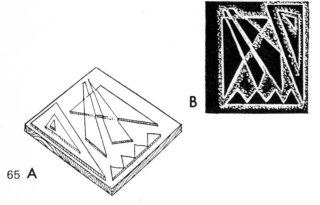

B

65 A

4. (Figure 65.) Shapes cut from varying thicknesses of scrap, pieces of card, cardboard, hardboard, corrugated paper, embossed wallpaper, thick felt, etc. are glued onto a backboard (A). The shapes may be built up or allowed to cross over each other. A leather punch may then be used to texture the shapes or the edges before glueing. Allow to dry, and print as before (B).

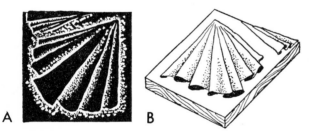

66 A   B

5. (Figure 66.) Pleated prints are formed from pieces of fairly thick cloth such as canvas or hessian, which are folded, pressed and glued onto a background block (B). Parts are built up into definite folds and ridges and then pressed lightly and left to dry. Print as before (A).

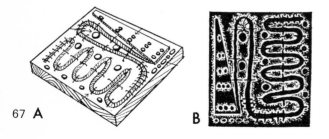

67 A   B

NOTE—Where appropriate a hand tacker, stapler, pins, nails, tacks, etc. may be used in any of the previous experiments in place of the glue (Figure 67A). The marks made by the staples, etc. when the block is printed can be used in the design (Figure 67B).

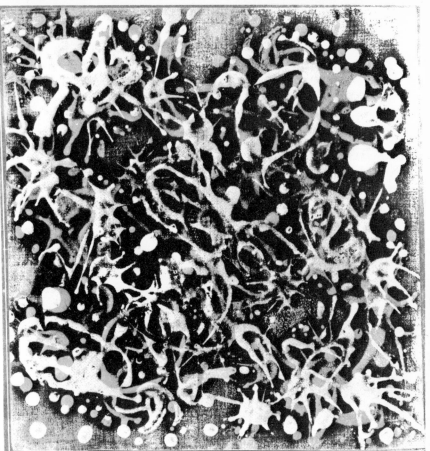

68

6. (Figure 68.) An interesting variation in this method of printing is to dye the piece of fabric a plain colour with a Dylon dye, allow to dry, and then to paint the pad with a *weak* solution of household bleach (Parazone, Domestos, etc.) and print the block on the dyed background with the diluted bleach. This will give a discharge pattern on a darker background. The example shown was printed from a block as in Figure 60.

The method is as follows—Mix 5 parts water–1 part bleach and paint pad. Avoid getting bleach on hands, clothes, etc. Whilst the print is still damp, cover with several layers of kitchen paper and press over with a hot iron. The white pattern will then appear. Rinse thoroughly and dry.

NOTE—Paper for this purpose should be used only once, and thrown away immediately after use.

7. (Figure 69.) Another, simpler form of discharge is where the piece of fabric (e.g. 1 ft. square) is dyed in a solution of 1 teaspoonful of potash dissolved in 1 quart of hot water. This should be done as quickly and completely as possible, rinsed in cold water, dried, ironed and then printed from a pad which has been painted with lemon juice. After the printed areas have turned to white, rinse through again, iron, and print on top with the dyestuffs as required. Example from a macaroni print, as Figure 62.

69

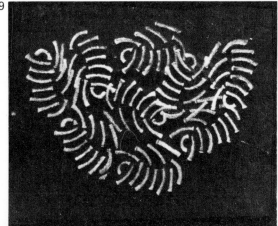

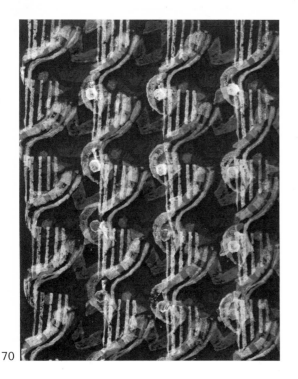

70

8. (Figure 70.) It is also possible to employ the antipathy between Procion M dyestuffs and vegetables, containing starch, particularly potatoes. If a piece of material is dyed in a Procion M dye, and, *before* fixation, is printed with the wetted half of a potato, the starch in the potato will affect the dyestuff and will give a form of discharge.

Similarly, a potato may be pressed on a pad, wetted with clean cold water or with a thin household starch mixture, and then printed all over a piece of fabric in a regular pattern. When dry, it is dyed in a Procion M dyebath in the normal manner without too much stirring, allowed to fix and rinsed. Again, the resist quality will be apparent after rinsing and drying.

NOTE—The section on discharge prints also gives the details for the use of Formosul, a chemical bleaching agent extensively used in fabric printing.

 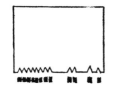 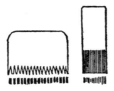

A

71   Various types of combs. A—from left to right, thin hard plastic; thick card, varnish or rub with a wax polish after cutting; rubber graining comb; metal graining comb (these last two may be purchased from paint and hardware stores). B—the working space.

B

9. (Figures 71 and 72.) Combed prints require pieces of hardboard, lino, plastic bags or tiles, or may be done direct on the table covering. Combs can be of the metal or rubber type as used by house decorators for graining, pieces of an ordinary comb, or made from pieces of cardboard or thick plastic (Figure 71A).

The first type is prepared by ironing the fabric flat and square upon the printing surface. About 2 in. of Lawrence's fabric ink is squeezed out onto a tile or plastic bag and rolled out with a lino roller. This is then rolled evenly all over a flat, uncut piece of lino or hardboard.

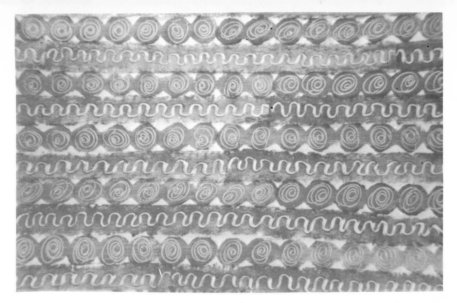

72 A

Next, a comb is used to make a pattern on the inked block (Figure 71B), which is then placed face downwards on the piece of fabric, and bumped with the rubber end of a printing mallet held upright or pressed firmly by hand.

The block is then carefully lifted off, re-inked, recombed and reprinted as required. Clean up with paraffin.

The block may also be printed using Polyprint and a $1\frac{1}{2}$-in. paint brush to apply it to the lino. It is then combed and printed as above, and cold water is used for cleaning up. When dry, iron the print to fix (Figure 72A).

An alternative method using Polyprint is to paint the dye directly onto the table covering or tile, etc. and make the pattern with the comb. The fabric is carefully placed on top, covered with newspaper and either gently rubbed by hand, or rolled with a clean fabric roller. When the fabric has been peeled off the table, it is dried and fixed as usual. Clean up with water (Figure 72B).

NOTE—only use sufficient dye to print, avoid 'coating' the fabric.

72 B

10. Tin printing is an unorthodox technique to produce lines on fabric without the usual overlaps or joins which can appear between prints from blocks or screens. The method is as follows:

The fabric is gummed down as before or fastened down with sellotape. The top and bottom of a small tin are cut out to leave smooth edges. The tin is placed beyond the sellotape edge, and held so that lower opening is pressed onto the table, then half filled with dye mixed to the consistency of the cream on top of the milk. Hold the tin firmly, keeping the lower opening tight to the table and slide it along the fabric. As it moves, it will leave a trail of dyestuff. This may be used in the production of printed hangings where curved and straight lines are required. Should it be necessary to stop a line in mid-fabric, place a piece of greaseproof paper on the fabric, slide the tin onto the paper and, whilst still firmly holding the tin, slide the paper and tin off the fabric onto the table top. Place a weight such as a block of wood on top of the tin to stop the dye leaking when not in use.

A tin with only one end cut out and with holes punched in the remaining end, can be used for producing separate stripes.

If straight lines are required down and/or across the fabric, lay a long splinter-free batten of wood on the fabric and use it to guide your hand, and the tin, in a completely straight line.

FURTHER SOURCES FOR MORE ADVANCED PAD PRINTING

Apart from the books mentioned in the General Bibliography the following are also recommended.

Print Making with a Spoon by N. Gorbaty, Reinhold, N.Y., 1960.
Plenty of ideas using the simplest materials.

Textile Printing and Painting Made Easy by U. Kuehnemann, Mills & Boon, London, 1967.
A small book full of ideas.

Fun with Fabric Printing by K. Monk, Mills & Boon, London, 1970.
Excellently explained techniques involving simple home-made equipment.

Printing for Fun by K. Ota, Museum Press, London, 1960.
Exceedingly well illustrated book of simple techniques.

BLOCK MAKING AND PRINTING

The development of simple Block printing has already been traced in the section on Pad printing. Apart from frescoes in a tomb at Beni Hasan circa 2,100 B.C. which seem to show costumes made of painted textiles, actual large wooden blocks for printing earth pigments on cloth are known to have been used by the Chinese around 200 B.C. and it is likely that they were in use much earlier. Certainly by the ninth century A.D. the Copts in Egypt were using such blocks and often decorating the print with gold and silver to produce 'tinsel' work on brilliantly coloured backgrounds of cotton or silk.

The techniques spread northward from the Mediterranean, various fabrics seemingly block printed have been found in Arles, France (A.D. 543); Durham, England (A.D. 1104) and Italy (thirteenth century). At the same time, examples from Peru show that the craft of block printing was well established before the Spanish conquest of the early sixteenth century.

The craft was extensively developed in Germany from the early Renaissance and also in India where a large export trade was built up through the various India Companies. This led to the establishment of block printing works in the Lowlands, Portugal, Germany, France, England, Switzerland and other places.

A great variety of printed textiles were produced for all kinds of purposes, although many of the wooden blocks were rather coarse in design. It was not until Bell developed roller printing with engraved copper plates that really fine designs were possible. Varieties included 'pin' and 'metal strip' blocks and 'mezzari' multi-blocks, all of which eventually gave way to roller printing. At this time too, the old vegetable dyes gave way to the newer synthetic dyes such as 'mauveine' discovered by Perkin in 1856 by distillation from coal tars. Many of these new dyes were very crude. This, together with a general deterioration in design, caused a number of designer craftsmen, in particular William Morris, to attempt a revival of hand-block printing, using many of the long discarded natural dyestuffs. Other groups of craftsmen artists such as Phyllis Barron and Dorothy Larcher working in Painswick and Roger Fry and the Omega workshops, and various craftsmen guilds continued the hand block methods, although such products cannot compete with machine techniques in the matter of costs.

73 Textile print attributed to the lower Rhine district with Byzantine motifs, 12th or 13th century. *After Forrer and courtesy CIBA Review.*

74 'Lea', a block print on cotton by William Morris *c.* 1883. *Courtesy Victoria and Albert Museum.*

As a craft in schools and colleges, Block printing is less flexible than other methods of decorating fabrics. The relative toughness of the lino requires greater control in the cutting of the design than is needed with potatoes or other vegetables. Lino or wood blocks, however, are not only more permanent but permit relatively fine cutting upon small or large areas.

Similarly, screen printing allows very free experimenting before the design needs to be fixed to the screen. The blocks may be printed directly with printing inks or may be printed from pads with thinned inks or any of the dyestuffs mentioned after the block surface has been prepared by sandpapering or flocking.

BASIC EQUIPMENT AND METHODS
Blocks

The block for printing can be made from wood and the wood most commonly used is sycamore. It is constructed in layers to prevent warping. These blocks although more permanent are costly to produce and require considerable skill in cutting. They *do not* require flocking when used with dyes as the wood is naturally absorbent. Wood blocks were often combined with small pins and thin brass or copper strips were inserted into the block to give very fine dots and lines.

However, it is now customary for most craftsmen to use lino. This is obtainable from many large stores as 'offcuts' or 'trimmings' which have been left over from contract furnishing. Lino should be plain and smooth. Inlaid, cork, or lino cloth are not suitable. The lino should be about $\frac{1}{8}$-in. thick.

75

A recent alternative is a cheap rubber sheet called 'Double-life' made in three thicknesses of flexible rubber in a variety of sizes which may be printed flat or fastened to a larger roller. It is also possible to cut designs on both sides employing very fine lines with the usual lino tools and to use water or oil-based dyes or inks (Figure 75).

75

Lino blocks may be used unmounted, although it is easier to handle larger or heavily cut blocks if the lino is mounted, to prevent too much movement during the printing. Thick cardboard is suitable for blocks up to 3 by 3 in. and hardboard, waterproof plywood or blockboard for larger blocks. The lino should be the same size as the backing and a waterproof glue of the impact type used to glue them together. This is best done before cutting the design.

To cut the lino to size, mark out with a pencil on the top plain surface using a 90° set square to obtain right angle corners. (To assist in the future printing and ensure easy and accurate registration of the block on the fabric it is essential that corners meant to be square are really 90°.) Place a steel cutting ruler on the portion of the lino required for the block, score a cut (there is no need to cut all the way through the lino) with a cutting knife, crack the lino along the score and cut through the cloth backing.

Tools

Two types of tools are available for the cutting of the design in the lino. Boxes containing a variety of cutting nibs, fitting into one handle, are often supplied for use in schools. But these are not usually strong enough for much vigorous cutting or clearing out. A much stronger tool is of the type shown in Figure 76A. A wide variety of gouge and V-tools are available (B), of which a useful basic selection would be gouge No. 11 (for background

76 A—V-tool in a small graver handle supplied in two qualities. B—T. N. Lawrence supplies a range of V-tools and gouges in the sizes shown.

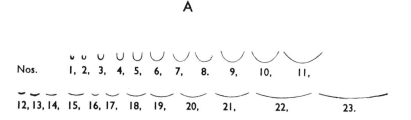

clearing out), V-tools No. 9 (thin lines) and No. 11 (wider, deeper lines). If needed these could be supplemented by gouge No. 6 and V-tool No. 8 together with a good sharp cutting knife. These tools are not toys but exceedingly sharp and care must be taken when using them. Figure 77 shows the type of roller (A) and mallet (B) recommended. (Diagrams by courtesy of T. N. Lawrence & Son Ltd.)

77 A—a printing roller. The most suitable sort of roller is made from soft transparent plastic which is more durable than gelatine or rubber, is suitable for use with oil or water colour inks and may be cleaned with turps, paraffin or water. It should be rested on back as shown when not in use. B—fabric printing mallet with rubber base. It is used the way shown, the *rubber* is bounced on the back of the block.

Designing

The section on sources for design work on page 108 will help at this stage. Try to design within the limits of a lino tool and not a pencil or brush. It is often best to forget colour in the first designs but instead to design in white poster colour and waterproof black Indian ink on a mid-grey or neutral paper. In this way the grey, white or black may be easily translated into any colours or tones of one colour. It is also possible to use pencil and a black ball point pen or a black felt tipped marker on white paper. Design within the same proportions that you propose for the finished print.

Cutting the Design

Experiment on scrap lino with various tools. Work at a table facing towards the light. Hold the lino tool as shown in Figure 78. If possible press the far end of the lino against something rigid. Push the lino tool into the lino but at first keep the top corners of the cutting edges above the lino surface or you will obtain ragged broken edges to the cut.

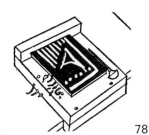

78

Remember, always cut *away* from the other hand that is holding the lino, **never**, please, **never**, towards your hand or yourself. Turn the block and not the tool. Lino tools go very deeply if they slip so take great care to instruct students as to their correct use.

After preparing the design, transfer it to the lino either by using carbon paper or by re-drawing direct onto the lino. If the final print is to be the same way round as the design, then reverse the carbon under the design and carbon onto the back of the design paper, then turn design paper over, replace carbon correctly and trace the reversed carbon drawing through onto the lino surface.

Alternatively, the design may be traced onto tracing paper which is reversed and used with carbon onto the lino.

Go over this drawing on the lino with a black waterproof Indian ink line. Allow to dry and cut away everything you do not wish to print in the first colour. Brush off small pieces of scrap lino and the block is ready to print.

Printing Table
This can be as described on page 9.

A suggested exercise is shown in Figure 79. Use the medium V-tool (Lawrence's V9) to cut around the letter and inside the square (A); the large gouge (Lawrence's G11) may be used to clear out the background (B). There is no need to expose the backing when clearing small spaces. The V11 tool may also be used with the V9 to cut out a letter (C).

Similarly, experiment with dots, dashes, circles (D) reversed letters (E) and other trial cuttings.

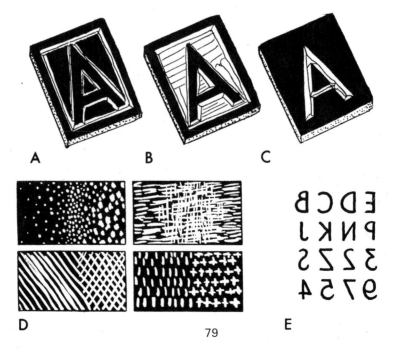

A   B   C

D   E

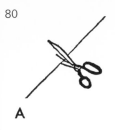

A

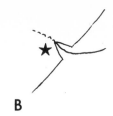

B

Preparation of Fabric

For trial prints any smooth plain fabric such as old sheets, pillowcases, and cheap calico will be quite satisfactory. These should all be slightly larger than the print.

For finished prints refer to page 150 for suitable fabrics and, either gum or sellotape the fabric lengths down onto the table or trim to size for table mats, cushion covers, etc. In the latter cases allow at least 1 in. all round for eventual hemming, fringing, etc. Figure 80 shows snipping an edge (A) and drawing a thread (B) and, in (C) various ways of dividing a square yard of fabric for table mats.

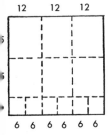

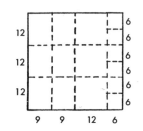

80   Cutting to a thread. A—cut $\frac{1}{4}$ in. from selvedge. B—pull a thread from cut and, while holding fabric at * with one hand gently pull the thread with the other hand. If the thread breaks cut on drawn thread, redraw the thread and so on. C—economical division of a square yard of fabric for table mats etc.

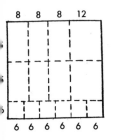

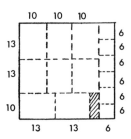

Gumming down, marking out and registration

It is always best to gum lengths of fabric down on the table as described on page 96. Mark out with fine threads stretched across the fabric and fastened to the table with sellotape. Do not use ball-point pens or felt markers as these are very difficult to wash out. The threads will give corner keying points and keep the prints in regular sequence or allow the pattern to be printed in stripes.

Mark the back of the block to show the top (or one side in a regular pattern). This will prevent misprints or allow the regular turning of the block during printing.

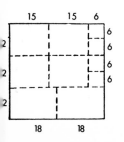

C

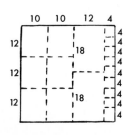

81 An iron nipping press in which is inserted a stiff bottom board, about one yard long by slightly less than the width of the press; on this lies a $\frac{1}{4}$ in. to $\frac{1}{2}$ in. pad of thick felt of same dimensions; next one piece of strawboard also the same size; then a pad of uncreased newspaper as thick as is required to obtain a good print; lastly a top stiff-board. Bottom and top boards could be old drawing boards, blockboard, $\frac{3}{8}$th play etc. Any imperfections in any of these such as cracks, dried paint blobs, folded paper, joins in felt will all tend to produce marks on the print.

Printing with fabric inks

Use a large tin lid, a flat tile, a piece of American cloth, or a thick polythene bag or PVC sheet on which to roll out the printers ink. Squeeze out 2 in. of ink from the tube and roll out with a lino roller. When the roller is evenly inked, roll out onto the lino but without excessive pressure. When the lino is covered with an even coating of ink it can be printed onto a piece of scrap cloth or paper in three different ways:

(1) Table mats and other small single items may be printed in a nipping press (Figure 81) which will give almost perfect prints. The quality of the print may be varied by increasing the amount of newspaper *under* the fabric and so allowing the block to bite more deeply into the fabric.

(2) If no press is available it is possible to obtain very good prints of mats by placing the block in the correct position on the fabric, and applying normal hand pressure. Then turning the block over, taking care not to disturb the fabric and either running a clean lino roller over the back of the fabric or rubbing with a bowl of a wooden spoon.

(3) An alternative method is to place the inked block face down onto the fabric which has been spread out on a piece of clean newspaper on the printing table. The back of the block is then bumped with the rubber end of a fabric printing mallet held upright.

When you feel the print is complete you are ready to 'pull' the cloth or paper from the block. Do this very carefully, checking to see that the print has taken by lifting only a corner at first and seeing if there is sufficient inking. If not, lift away about half of the print, carefully roll more ink on the point exposed, replace print and repeat printing process as above. After making a good trial print repeat the whole process upon the good fabric. Add another 1 in. or so, as required, of ink to the tile after each third or fourth print or as seems necessary. Care must be taken not to put out *too much* ink or lines will become blocked with ink.

Table mats and other small items should be pinned up to dry overnight.

Ink must be cleaned up with paraffin. If ink is left to dry on rollers, blocks or tiles it will be most difficult to remove and will make further printing difficult or impossible.

If a second or further colours are to be used any necessary cutting should be done and the block printed directly on top of the first colour (Figure 82). Take care to place the block exactly on top of the previous print. Do this by gently placing one corner in position, lowering one long edge to the next corner, and then the remainder of the block.

Clean up, dry prints and fringe, hem, etc. as required (see also Plate 7, page 58).

In multi-colour printing of this type, the block is not available for further printing unless a new first block is cut. It is essential to make a large enough 'first edition' for immediate needs.

Although printing ink is quite satisfactory for table mats and other small articles that remain flat in use, it invariably stiffens the fabric and cannot be satisfactorily used for fabrics which are required to be draped or to hang. For these particular purposes a pigment colour may be used, although again there is a slight stiffening with fine fabrics since pigment colours coat rather than stain.

82 Printing a second colour on a first print. Hold inked lino block at points CC; drop on to corner A; lower to corner B keeping edge AB level with print edge; then lower rest of block on to print.

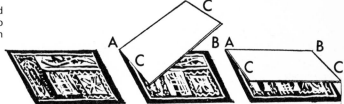

83 Masking out parts of a block. This not only saves ink but allows one to cut and print a part of the lino *at the second print* upon the original cloth. In the example here a large block is masked to allow only a small part to be printed as a small glass mat. A—the original lino block; B—a paper print from this block with a 4-in. square cut out (i.e. star shape) and then a 5-in. square (i.e. wavy border area); C—a 6-in. square is drawn on the back of the paper print. D—lino block is inked with a new colour over, say, 9 in. square on bottom right corner; large paper print and 4-in. square placed in position and a 6-in. square mat placed so as to print exposed border.

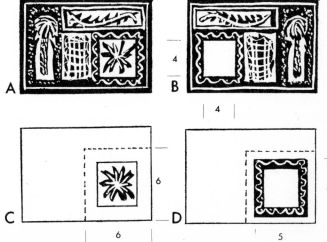

For true dyestuffs (acid, direct, reactives, etc.), the printing pad described on page 52 is quite suitable. It should be large enough to accommodate the block at one pressing. A more professional pad may be prepared as in Figure 84. This will not ruck up during printing and so will transfer the dye evenly to the block surface.

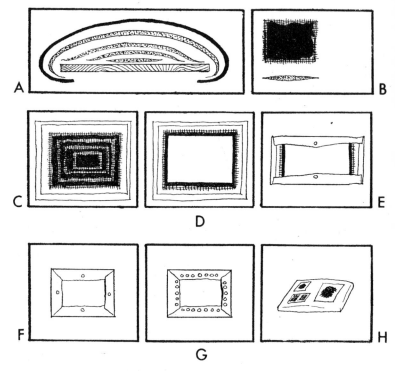

84 Materials required—1 piece of blockboard, say, 12 by 18 in., 4 pieces of carpet underfelt (5 by 11 in., 7 by 13 in., 10 by 16 in., 14 by 20 in.); 1 piece of white felt 16 by 20 in.; 1 piece of thick plastic or oil cloth 18 by 24 in.; drawing pins or hand tacker.

A—section of a dye pad. B—fray edges of each piece of underfelt. C—place plastic down on table, place white felt on top, place frayed pieces of underfelt on top—largest first, smallest last. D—place blockboard on top. E—pull up one edge of plastic and white felt and pin or tack on to blockboard, pull up opposite edges, stretch taut and pin, staple or tack (f). G—check front is smooth, complete pinning. H—as well as being used for large printing pads a number of small pads may also be used.

If this dye pad is cleaned after use it will last for many years.

The pieces of white felt or absorbent cloth used as printing pads can be cut to 18 by 24 in. and pinned on to back of block to avoid damaging plastic covering.

Plain lino surface is not particularly suitable for water based dyes as lino contains a large amount of oil itself. The resulting print is often mottled or patchy in quality. This can be overcome by several methods:

(1) The *lino block* is pressed down against a sheet of No. 2 (medium) sandpaper on a flat surface and heavy pressure used in a circular motion to cover the lino surface with fine scratches. This will allow the lino to pick up and hold the dye.

(2) The traditional but rather laborious method is to apply, after cutting the design, a coat of flocking to the lino surface previously prepared with a coating of mordant (Figure 85). This requires renewing as the flock wears off, but the resulting felt-like texture holds the dye. If reactive dyes are to be used, then the mordant must be replaced with Bedafin 2001 and after the flock has been applied the block is placed in an ordinary oven for five minutes at 135°C. It can also be replaced with an adhesive such as Clam, Bostik 2 (UK) or Sobo (USA).

(3) Another alternative is the use of the 'Double-life' flexible rubber sheet already mentioned.

Lino blocks may be used to print wallpaper using inks, pigment dyes or Procion M range reactive dyes. The surface may be protected by an aerosol matt protective spray.

Plain coloured paper serviettes are also useful for lino block printing, using inks or dyes as for wallpaper.

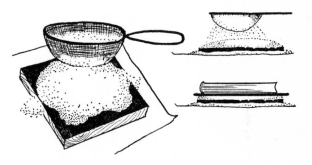

85 Flocking a block so that it will pick up and hold water-based dyes. A thin coat of mordant is rolled on to the lino block (standing on a large piece of card or paper) and a coat of flock dusted on through a sieve. It is important to use only dry flocking and to coat on quite a thick ($\frac{1}{4}$ in.) layer. A piece of card larger than the lino is then placed on top of this and a book on top of that to *gently* press the whole for 12–24 hours. When the mordant is dry the surplus flock is removed by holding the block vertically over the backing paper or card and tapping the back of the block. The whole process is then repeated and after a further 12–24 hours and removal of surplus flock the resulting felt-like texture will hold water-based dyes. Surplus flock may be saved and used again and again as long as it is kept dry. With care in use the block will last for a long time. When the flock is worn off in patches the block may be lightly sandpapered until evenly surfaced and then reflocked as above. Wash off surplus dye after use in cold water, dry by slotting on newspaper and store away from excessive heat.

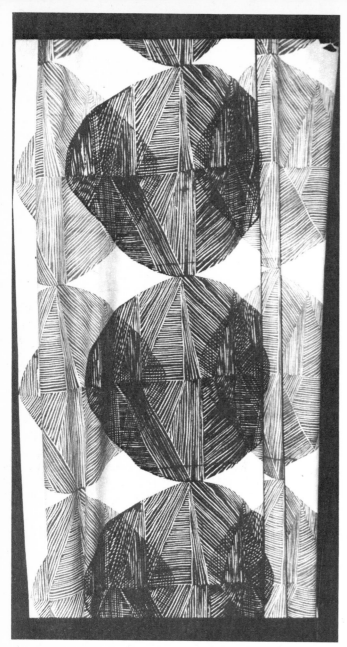

86 Block print using Direct dyes on cotton. Unit of design size 15 in. square. *Coventry College of Education.*

FURTHER SOURCES FOR MORE ADVANCED BLOCK PRINTING

Apart from the books mentioned in the General Bibliography the following are also recommended:

Block Printing on Textiles by J. Erickson, Watson-Guptill, N.Y., 1961.

Wood-Block Printing by F. M. Fletcher, Pitman, London N.D.

Creative Print Making by P. Green, Batsford, London, 1964.

Introducing Surface Printing by P. Green, Batsford, London, 1967.

Although both these books are concerned with paper printing many of the techniques and design ideas are very interesting.

Printmaking a medium for basic design by P. Weaver, Studio Vista, London, 1968.

Although mainly concerned with paper printing this book has many very original techniques.

SUPPLIERS OF BLOCK PRINTING MATERIAL
Great Britain

Dryad Handicrafts—Northgates, Leicester for lino, tools, inks, etc.

T. N. Lawrence & Son Ltd—2 Bleeding Heart Yard, Greville Street, Hatton Garden, London E.C.1, for lino and wood blocks, tools, rollers, inks, flocking, unusual printing papers, etc.

The Sutcliffe Moulded Rubber Co. Ltd—Ossett, Yorkshire, for "Double-life", a rubber 'lino' for use flat or from a roller. Fabrics—see page 151. Dyes—see page 123.

USA

American Crayon Co.—Sandusky, Ohio. *J. Johnson*—51 Manhasset Avenue, Manhasset, New York.

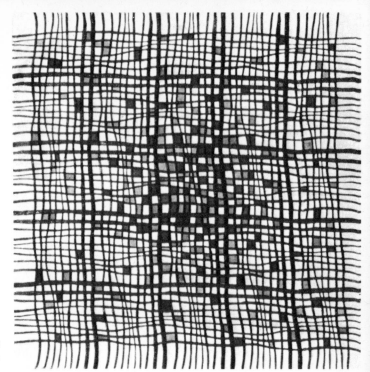

87A Block printed silk scarf using acid dyes with handfilled in colours. *Designed by Margaret Holgate, printed by Patricia Robinson.*

87B Block printed silk scarf using Direct dyes. *Designed by Margaret Holgate, printed by Patricia Robinson.*

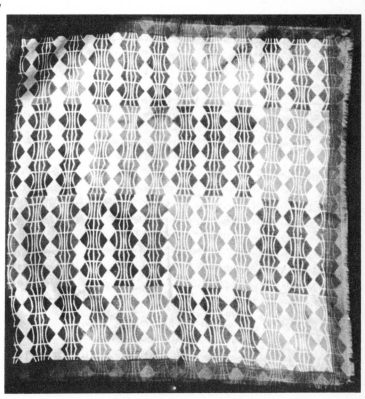

SCREEN MAKING AND PRINTING

Screen printing has many advantages over other methods of fabric printing. Industrially it provides a simple, quick and far less costly method than that of printing with engraved metal rollers. It is based upon the early Japanese 'Yuzen' form in which a stencil was cut out of a special rice paper. In the earliest form the free parts were held in place by human hairs. This later developed into a method whereby the complete stencil was mounted upon a fine mesh silk. The basic idea remained undeveloped for many centuries and it was not until the beginning of the present century that its potential as a commercial art technique was foreseen. It was still later, that its possibilities as a method of printing textiles were realized and developed.

The technique of screen printing is one that is particularly adaptable at experimental level for junior, middle and secondary school students. At advanced level it enables the student to experiment freely, with very simple and inexpensive materials, in the development of form, design, colour and texture.

88 'Osborne', a contemporary screen print. *Designed by David Bartle for the Young Sanderson Fabric Collection. Inspired by the Art Nouveau revival. Courtesy Sanderson Fabrics.*

In its present form screen printing in schools and colleges consists of a rectangular wood (or metal) frame across which a fine woven material has been tightly stretched. This material is often a medium-mesh silk but can be terylene, nylon, organdie or even fine mesh metal fabric. Parts of this material are blocked out with a filler that will not be affected by the kind of dye or ink to be used.

The principle is that these filled-in parts of the screen prevent the dye from reaching the fabric. In this way the dye or ink is forced through the unblocked parts of the screen so as to print corresponding shapes upon the fabric.

BASIC EQUIPMENT
A simple frame (Figure 89)

Frames of about 12 by 10 in. outside measurement for children to use, or of about 15 by 13 in. outside measurement for older students will give printing areas of 6 by 6 in. and 9 by 9 in. respectively. The frame should be made from an ordinary 2 by 1-in. planed softwood which will keep its shape without warping although in and out of water during use. Straight grained, knot-free beech or sycamore is excellent (A).

Although the corners must be square, it is not necessary to make complicated corner joints. The simplest joints are quite strong enough for normal use, provided that 2-in. length oval nails and waterproof glue are used. The corners may be butt jointed, glued and pinned with 2-in. oval nails (or holes drilled and 2-in. screws used) or fixed with corrugated fasteners, or halving jointed or shoulder jointed and nailed and glued as before (B).

The completed frame should lie flat against a flat surface. All outside edges and corners must be well bevelled with coarse sandpaper and the whole frame smoothed down with fine sandpaper so that no rough or sharp parts are left to catch the organdie or other covering.

It is advisable to make most screens of the same size and squeegees to fit; this will economize in the numbers required.

89

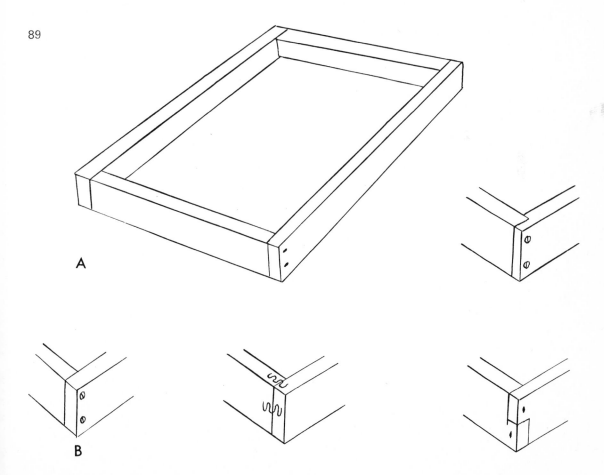

A

B

Covering the frame (Figure 90)

Bolting Silk (grade 8XX is most useful), terylene (grade 8TT) and nylon (grade 85NN) are all exceedingly durable and are extensively used in commercial screen printing. Silk is usually far too expensive for experimental use in schools. The most common substitute is cotton organdie, obtainable either from any screen printing suppliers, or general art and craft materials suppliers. Take care that the organdie is specified for screen printing, as some dressmakers' organdie is of too fine a mesh to allow the dye to pass through. Proceed as follows:

Cut the organdie 4 in. wider and 4 in. longer than the outside screen measurement. Fold or iron 1 in. in, all round (A); wet the organdie and spread over the frame (B). Pin through the double edge or organdie at the centre of one side (marked 1 in C). Continue pinning in the order shown, pulling the organdie evenly outwards and keeping the edges level with the frame edge.

Turn the frame round and pin the opposite side in the same manner (D), pulling the organdie across the frame as well as outwards. Before *each* pinning, stretch the organdie as taut as possible to give a flat, drum-like surface. Keep the threads of the organdie parallel to the edges of the frame.

Continue in the same manner with sides 3 and 4, again keeping the threads and edges parallel, and tucking in the corners neatly (E).

Examine the frame and if there is any sign of twisting, reinforce the corners with metal corner plates (F). It is of course possible to tack or staple the organdie, but drawing pins are easier to remove if this should ever be necessary.

90

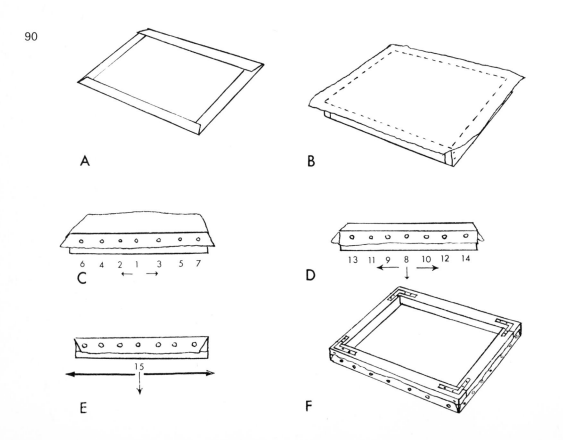

A

B

6 4 2 1 3 5 7
C

13 11 9 8 10 12 14
D

15
E

F

A simple squeegee (Figure 91)

For pressing the colour through the screen, a squeegee is required.

The simplest, cheapest and most efficient is the handled type (A) such as the 'Marvel Squeegeasy', designed for use in cleaning windows, but excellent for all forms of screen printing. The more traditional type is the one shown in (B) and these may be purchased complete and ready to use. Examples shown are supplied by Ashworth-Lyme Marquetry. Use vee-edged for blotch and square-edged for fine line work. The protruding rubber shoulders enable one to rest the squeegee on the edges of the screen when not in use.

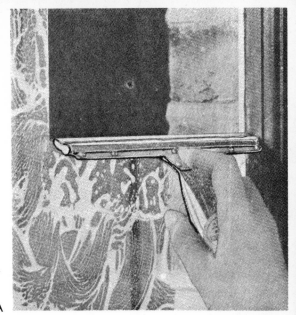

91 A

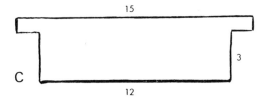

C

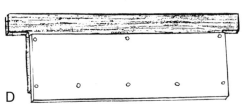

D   B

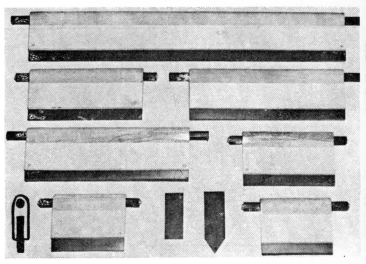

It is, however, easy to make these yourself from relatively cheap materials. A piece of hardboard may be cut to the shape shown (C), with the blade about 1 in. smaller than the inside screen measurement, and three essentials observed:

(1) all edges smoothed
(2) corners rounded
(3) the blade edge must be straight. A refinement is to fasten a length of rubber draught excluder or stripping along the blade edge, using an Impact (GB) or Sobo (USA) adhesive (D).

Another type (E) is made from a sandwich of, say, 2 by $\frac{1}{4}$ in. strip squeegee rubber between two pieces of strip wood, with a further wood strip handle nailed on, so that the squeegee may be rested on the screen edges. Squeegee rubber may be bought by the foot from any silk screen suppliers.

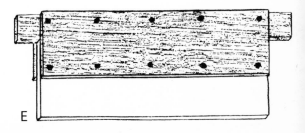

E

Masking the screen (Figure 92)

Again a variety of methods may be employed to block out the edges of the screen and so provide a place to hold a reservoir of dye between screenings.

Method 1. Firstly, a pencil oblong is drawn inside the screen (A), parallel to the edges. It should leave a *minimum* 1-in. margin at the sides and 2 in. at the top and bottom to provide the dye 'reservoirs' already mentioned. The margins may be filled in by using exterior quality clear varnish (B).

Turn the screen over and completely varnish the margins (NOT the centre oblong) and the outside of the frame with a thin layer of varnish. Do not use too much varnish or it will form drips on the inside of the screen as it dries. Allow to dry. Turn the frame over and varnish the insides of frame and the organdie, again leaving the centre oblong unvarnished. Leave to dry. Hold the frame up to the light; if any pinholes are visible in the margins where the varnish has not taken, then touch up with more varnish. Leave to dry. This method gives a permanent yet transparent blocking out and also strengthens the screen where it joins the frame.

Method 2. Use gumstrip (the gum of which has been well soaked) on the underside, being sure to overlap the strips by $\frac{1}{2}$ in. and take up the edge of frame (C). When dry, the inside margins of the screen can be further sealed by a coat of varnish or hot candle wax. Certain types of thin PVC cloth masking strips with a self adhesive waterproof glue are also useful.

Method 3. An alternative but less permanent method is to block out the margins with hot candle wax which will last for a number of prints before breaking down and allowing the dye to penetrate. Such leaks can however be easily touched up with fresh hot wax.

92

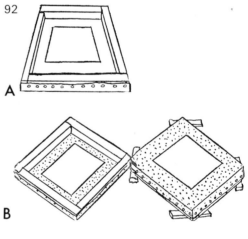

A

B

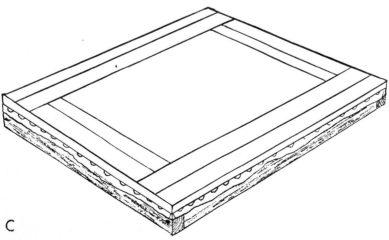

C

93 Screen printing by hand. Note: threads across fabric to assist registration; 'Marvel Squeegeasy' type of squeegee; slotted metal angle construction of tables with wood 'sleepers' on top and blockboard tops covered with felt blanket and plastic covering; 'Star' type steamer in background, brush racks on far window-ledge. *Coventry College of Education, photograph by P. W. and L. Thompson, Coventry.*

STARTING TO PRINT
The working area (Figure 93)
In Screen printing on fabric, it is important to have the working area and procedure well organized before the actual printing commences. A suggested table layout is shown. In addition, a clothes horse and/or a clothes line with pegs (pins) or bull-dog paper clips will be necessary to take finished work.

The dyes
Provided that the consistency is correct (i.e. the dye used is not so thick that it will not go through the mesh, or so thin it floods under the blocked-out parts of the screen; and it does not dry in the screen whilst in use and so block up the open mesh), almost any mixture of colouring and thickener may be used.

There are two main types of dyes available for screen printing.

The Emulsion (not Emulsion *paint* of course but emulsified dyes) or Pigment type of which a number of proprietary brands are on the market, is not really a true dyestuff since it coats the fibre rather than achieving the penetration and complete chemical interlocking of a true dye. For the beginner, an Emulsion dye such as Polyprint (GB), Printex (GB), Aquaprint (USA) or Prang (USA) is excellent. It is simple to mix and when the dye is dry, it is easily fixed on the fabric by ironing. In addition, it only requires cold water and a little detergent to clean up the screens, squeegees and all the other apparatus used.

As the solvent used in Emulsion dyes will dry out over a period of time, any mixed dye should be kept in screw-topped jars, although it is preferable to mix only sufficient for immediate use.

The true dyestuff is the other type of dye such as the Procion and Cibacron Reactive dyestuffs, the Direct, Acid and many other chemical dyestuffs, and also, of course, natural dyestuffs, which are available under almost innumerable trade names and classes. We have classified the most useful in the section dealing with Recipes on page 123. For school work we recommend the Procion M range which is easy to mix, does not require expensive chemicals, or any elaborate fixation process, and is cleaned up with cold water. This range represents a relatively simple method of producing bright shades, fast to washing and light, on cotton, linen and viscose rayon fabrics.

For printing on paper, either for poster work or during experiments with pattern shapes, 3 parts ordinary school tempera powder paint or 'Brusho' colour may be well mixed with 2 parts of cold water to a thin paste consistency, $\frac{1}{4}$ part glycerine and $\frac{1}{2}$ part of soap flakes added. The whole is blended to the consistency of thin cream, without any undissolved specks of paint left to cause streaks.

An alternative recipe only requires cellulose wallpaper paste, mixed slightly thicker than maker's instructions to which is added any colouring matter such as household dye powder, dissolved in a little warm water (obtainable from most stores), coloured school ink powder, Indian ink, stains or even cocoa, coffee powder, dandelion leaf extract, blue bag liquor and similar unusual compounds, all of which give ample opportunity for inexpensive experiments. Obviously the compounds given here for paper printing are not fast enough to be of use in serious fabric printing, where the final product must be washable and reasonably fast to light.

Common faults, causes and remedies
(Figure 94)
The first few prints from a screen are often rather poor until the screen has been 'run in'.

Here are a few of the common faults and how to correct them:
(A) Unwanted spots of colour around the pattern, or where the dye should *not* penetrate.
Pinholes have obviously developed in the masking, and should be touched out with a spot of varnish or hot wax.
(B) Patchy print.
This is caused by
either insufficient dyepaste to cover the pattern area completely during printing, so add more dyepaste to the screen,
or the dyepaste is too thick, and a little more water or binder (whichever is used in recipe) should be added to the dyepaste;

or an uneven printing surface;
or a warped frame.
(C) The spreading of dyepaste outside the design, often as 'runs' of colour.
This is a result of
either too thin a dyepaste, in which case thicken it slightly,
or ridges or lumps of varnish, wax, etc., on the underneath of the printing part of the screen which prevent flat contact between the screen and table; remove or smooth down these lumps.
or the printing paper is not sufficiently absorbent. This particular fault often cures itself when the print is on cloth instead of paper.
or slack screen covering.
(D) Smudged print.
This is caused
either by movement of the screen during printing, which is easily remedied by holding the screen more firmly,
or the covering of screen (organdie, etc.), being too slack, and moving with the use of the squeegee. The only remedy for this, unfortunately, is to re-cover the screen more tightly.

(E) Dye marking-off on the print in the wrong places.
This is because
either the screen has picked up dye from being placed where it overlaps a print not yet dry. Wipe the dirty areas of the screen carefully, and mask prints with newspaper where the screen is likely to overlap;
or the screen has become dirty by being put down flat between prints, instead of being propped against a piece of wood as in Figure 95D, page 95).
(F) Clogging of the screen, giving a patchy print.
This is due
either to leaving the screen for too long a time between prints and allowing the dye or paint to dry in the screen and clog the mesh. In this case, soak the screen in cold water for a few moments, and wipe over after the dye has softened;
or the dyepaste being too thick for the size of mesh of the screen covering. To remedy, thin the dyepaste a little.

94 A

B

C

D

E

F

Cleaning up

Wear rubber gloves.

Always clean the screen as soon as possible after printing. After spooning out the unused dyepaste into a screw-topped jar, place the screen with underside to bottom of the sink and fill with cold water. Leave for a few moments and then clean with a *soft* brush, or if too large for the sink, place on a pad of newspaper, and wipe out with a wet cloth. In either case, ensure that no dye is left to block the screen. Wash the squeegee and any bowls, spoons, etc. in cold water.

If the dye is allowed to dry in the screen mesh, it is exceedingly difficult to remove. Only a long soaking in the solvent for the particular dyestuff used will be efficaceous. Sometimes it is necessary to resort to a paint remover such as Polystrippa.

95

SOME SIMPLE EXPERIMENTS

1. (Figure 95.) Cut some newspaper and old cloth (sheets etc.) to a size about the outside dimensions of the screen. Place one sheet of this printing newspaper on the printing pad.

Take a piece of greaseproof or tracing paper 1 in. larger all round than the centre oblong of the screen. Fold the greaseproof paper into quarters and cut out a pattern (A) which, when opened out, will be larger than the size of the centre oblong on the screen. Open it out and iron flat between newspapers. Place on top of the printing newspaper, then place the screen centrally on top of this. The greaseproof pattern should show through the centre oblong as through a window (B).

The dyepaste which, for this work, can be Polyprint or Printex (mixed with binder), Procion M range dye (thickened with Manutex RS 5% thickening), or the paint mixtures given on page 92, is spread evenly inside the screen along the nearest masked edge. Only sufficient dyepaste should be poured out for the particular pattern in hand. Hold the frame steady with one hand, place the squeegee in position between the dye and the frame edge, and with one firm stroke of the squeegee, push the dyepaste to the opposite side (C). Carefully place the squeegee behind the dyepaste, and pull back to the original position, clearing the paste from the pattern area. Keep the squeegee almost upright during printing. Afterwards, lift the screen carefully, commencing with one side first and after removal from the fabric prop the screen on the piece of wood (D). This keeps the dyepaste and squeegee at one end and prevents the wet screen from sticking to the table. Then examine the print and screen.

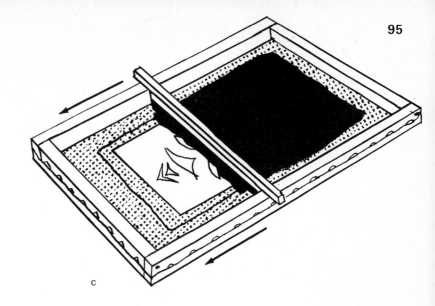

If the print is reasonable, try further prints on paper and then on cloth and fix the dye as required.

Using cold water, clean up the table top and all the equipment used as soon as possible.

2. (Figure 96.) Prepare the printing table as before. Mark the outline of the shape to be printed through the screen with a soft pencil (A). Place the cut or torn greaseproof or newspaper shapes on the marked-out shape (B). Place the screen on top of the shapes, and squeegee the dye through the screen (C). Lift the screen up, and not only will a design based on the shapes be printed on the under paper or fabric (D), but the shapes will be stuck to the underside of the screen ready for further printing.

It is possible to add further paper to the screen between screenings, and print back on top of the original in the same or a different colour. The screen may also be turned round and printed on top of the previous print. It may be printed a little away from the first print, or some of the paper removed and/or replaced. There is an infinite series of experiments possible with this method.

It is difficult to remove and replace or store paper shapes without distortion. It is simpler to cut two or three together before printing and save the others for future use.

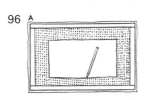

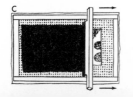

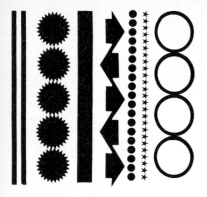

97

3. (Figure 97.) Other prepared paper shapes such as stars, reinforcement 'holes', brown paper, gumstrip, etc., may be used as masks to stop the dye from penetrating the screen mesh.

4. Use hot candle wax (melted in a double container such as a glue pot) to paint the design on the underside of the screen. Provided the screen has been cleaned first, wax may be added during the printing to vary the pattern or removed in part or completely, by ironing with a medium-hot iron between several sheets of newspaper.

5. Fine designs may be directly painted upon the underside of the screen with external grade transparent varnish or lacquer. When dry, they can be printed as already described.

Such 'varnish' designs can be difficult to remove completely from the screen unless a special solvent is obtained from the manufacturers of the particular varnish used.

6. All the above methods may be combined together in any way to produce the particular effect required.

MORE ADVANCED SCREEN PRINTING
Investment in some form of screen-stretching machine will pay dividends. Many printing faults arise from slack screens. A machine and the use of Terylene will prevent these.

Gumming down
All paper or fabric must be quite flat before it is printed—even ironed if neces-sary—or the resulting print will be streaky.

It is always advisable to gum down *fabric* to the table, so that it does not move during the printing, and is not lifted by the screen from the table on completion of a print. It is not necessary to stick paper to the table.

For experiments, it may only be neces-sary to attach the fabric to the table with small strips of sellotape at the edges, well clear of the pattern area.

For larger work, the fabric should be gummed down to the printing surface as follows:

A little mixed Manutex, thinned with water to the consistency of the top of the milk, should be spread with a soft, clean cloth and rubbed well in, so that the sur-face appears dry and no streaks of wet gum are visible as these would fill up the fibres, and prevent full absorption of the dye. It may also be applied with a squeegee to avoid streaks and blobs. Dry thoroughly. The fabric is then ironed to the printing surface with a medium-hot iron, taking care to keep the warp and weft threads at the correct angles. It is easier to start in the centre of one end and work outwards with the iron, making sure there are no 'bubbles' or creases left. Check that no loose threads have crept under the fabric, as these will affect the print adversely.

Marking out and registration
(Figure 98)
Never mark out with biros, felt pens, etc., as these will *not* wash out. Wherever pos-sible, avoid using pencils and chalk. Instead, use fine thread stretched across the fabric and fastened to the table with sellotape (A). This will give corner keying points within which the patterned area of the screen may be placed. If a pencil has to be used it is best to use a very soft

one (2B) and make faint dots or small corner crosses (B).

It is possible (depending on type of pattern) to obtain reasonable repeat printing 'by eye', but at times the use of deep colours will make it difficult to see through the transparent part of the screen.

Where a pattern is in bands or stripes, strips of newspaper may be laid at equidistant spaces across or down the fabric (trapped with sellotape if necessary) and the screen printed between them. In this way, equal spacing is easily maintained.

If a full repeat is marked out with threads all over the fabric, it is often advisable to print alternate shapes (to avoid the wet print marking off on the underneath of the screen and then re-marking onto the fabric) and when these are dry, to print the remainder (C). Otherwise, the first prints may be covered with newspaper until the entire screen is clear of them, or they may be dried with a portable convector heater before making a touching print.

METHODS

1. With this method there is no need to mask the edges of the screen with varnish, wax or masking tape, but the design must be confined to the central oblong or square as before.

Paint the *design*, using hot wax, on the underside of the central space and when cold use a large brush to coat the *whole* underside, frame edges and sides with

either (a) a PVC adhesive, soluble in water but waterproof when dry

or (b) a plastic emulsion or acrylic paint

or (c) gelatine and potassium dichromate as in (2) below.

When dry, apply a second coat and when this too is dry, check by holding the screen up to the light for any pinholes and touch out where necessary.

When the screen is completely blocked out and dry, in the case of (a) and (b) remove the wax by washing out with hot water. In the case of (c) it may also be ironed out between newspaper if this is easier. Use a medium-hot iron as described in (4) on page 96.

The disadvantage of methods (a) and (b) is that one cannot see through the blocked-out parts of the screen when printing.

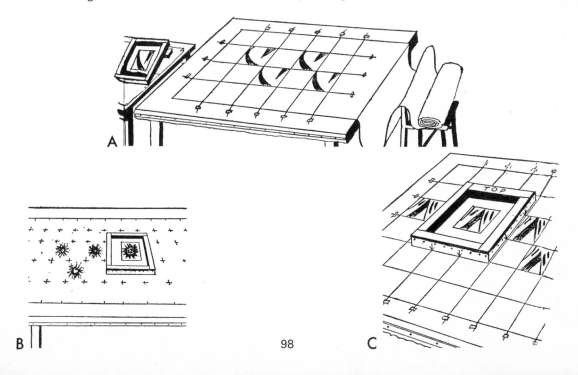

A

B

C

99 A

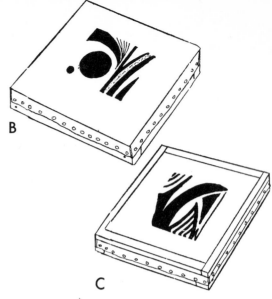

B

C

2. (Figure 99.) The 'photographic' method, using gelatine, potassium dichromate and a screen covered as before, but with the edges *not* masked with varnish. Care must be taken to work in a warm, draught-free room.

(a) Mix 1 part powdered cooking or photographic gelatine with 4 parts of cold water and dissolve in a double container over low heat. This takes about thirty minutes, *but remember the gelatine must not boil.*

(b) Hold the screen nearly vertical and, using a 2-in. paint brush, paint a *thin* layer of gelatine across the underside of the screen and right across the frame edges (A). Single, flowing strokes should be used as backward and forward strokes will cause bubbles which will adversely affect the process. Do not let the leading edge of the gelatine solidify, but avoid going over the parts already gelatined.

(c) Prop up to dry, away from direct sun or heat.

(d) Apply a second, similar coat on the reverse (inside); dry, then apply a third coat to the first side, and dry.

Three thin coats are much better than one thick one.

(e) Have the design drawn the correct size and way on the paper and place the screen upon this with the gelatined covering resting on the drawing. Draw the design on the inside of the screen in the correct central position, leaving sufficient space between the design and frame edges to hold the dye as in other methods.

(f) Turn the screen over and paint within the central space, the areas required to print (B). Use special screen lacquer or Japanese lacquer. Leave to dry. Hold up to the light, and touch out any pinholes in the lacquer. Allow to dry.

(g) Dissolve 1 part potassium dichromate in 10 parts slightly warm water. Leave to cool. Paint the outside of the dry screen and frame with this freshly-made, cold solution. Apply it very sparingly with a 2-in. paint brush over all the gelatine and lacquer. USE CAREFULLY—*it stains and is poisonous; throw away any left over.*

Prop the screen up in daylight but not full sun and leave until the unlacquered gelatine becomes deep nut brown. This will take up to one hour.

Wash out the brush immediately after use.

The lacquer will have protected the gelatine from the potassium dichromate and, even after the screen has been exposed to light, this protected gelatine will remain soluble in water. The gelatine directly painted with the potassium dichromate will have become completely insoluble in water.

Wash the screen in hot water to remove the lacquer and the gelatine under it, and when dry, the screen is then ready to print. Should any pinholes become apparent in the blocked out parts, touch out with a little hot wax. Provided the gelatine and potassium dichromate were painted right up to the outside of the screen, no further masking should be necessary. Some craftsmen strengthen the join inside between the frame and screen covering by placing a 2-in. strip of PVC cloth or gumstrip paper around the join (C).

3. (Figure 100.) A true photographic screen uses the same principles as the previous method but requires a lightproof room or large cupboard. It does provide the opportunity of making very detailed and accurate screens though. The more detailed the design, the finer the screen covering required to reproduce the detail. The method is relatively simple but requires care. The screen is first prepared by coating with gelatine as already described on page 98. The dry screen is now taken into a completely light-proof space with an orange safe light as the only source of illumination. Here it is quickly coated with a potassium dichromate solution. As this dries, so the gelatine will become exceedingly sensitive to light and must be kept in total darkness.

The design should be drawn in black poster colour on tracing paper. It can also be drawn in Photopake on Kodatrace or Ethulon photographic film. A piece of block or hardboard (C) should be cut to fit exactly inside the screen (B). Returning to the lightproof space, the piece of hardboard is then placed inside the screen and pushed right up against the inside of the covering and supported by building up inside the screen with books etc., so that the screen frame does not rest on the table and the hardboard is pressed tightly against the inside of the screen (D).

The design is now stuck underneath a piece of plate or heavy window glass using sellotape, and the glass and design placed in position on top of the screen (A). The whole assembly of blocks, hardboard, upsidedown screen, design, and glass is now placed either in daylight or under a bright artificial light. The gelatine under the black design will remain soluble in water and the rest will change to a deep nut brown. This will take about one hour, depending upon the strength of light available. Strong sunlight will only take about ten minutes, but dull daylight (or exposure 2 ft. from a 300 Watt lamp) will take up to two hours.

Immediately the exposed gelatine and dichromate mixture has changed to brown, the screen must be quickly taken away and washed in warm water. The unexposed gelatine will wash out leaving the screen ready to print after drying out. Again, the edges may be reinforced if so desired (page 90).

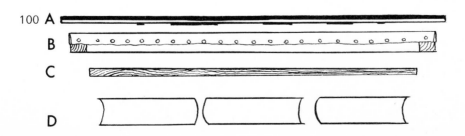

100

101   Screen print in one colour with direct dyes on cotton. *Jan Probin, Coventry College of Education.*

4. The 'Profilm' method of blocking out. This consists of a film of lacquer on a transparent backing sheet. The method of application is easy to follow and consists of placing the Profilm (lacquer side up) on top of the design and fixing with sellotape at corners. The design will show through, and the parts to be printed are cut out of the lacquer *only*, and peeled off. Care must be taken not to cut the backing sheet. The screen is then placed upon the sheet of Profilm, lacquer side to underside of the screen and a piece of tracing or grease-proof paper placed inside the screen. The lacquer of the Profilm is transferred to the screen by ironing on top of the paper with a warm iron. When the lacquer is set in the screen, the backing paper is carefully peeled off and the screen is ready for use.

When no longer required, the Profilm is removed from the screen by the use of methylated spirits. Place the part of the screen to be cleaned onto a pad of news-paper, pour in a little methylated spirits, cover with a single layer of newspaper, and allow to soak for a few minutes. Remove the newspaper, turn over the screen and peel off Profilm. Repeat this process until the printing area is clear.

It is easier to fix Profilm to cotton organdie than to nylon or terylene. These must be degreased as (c) in 5 following.

5. The photographic method using pro-prietary film. It enables any original negative or black and white drawing to be transferred to the screen surface and then printed upon paper, fabric or other sur-faces. A dark room is necessary and basic photographic materials.

(a) First select the photograph or design to be transferred to the screen. High con-trast of tone is useful. If photograph is a negative obtain a contact 'Positive' print on 'Kodalith' Ortho Film, Type 3, (35mm). Then use this (or, if original design was a positive, use that) and obtain a second

102 Screen printed table cloth and serviettes in two colours with reactive dyes on cotton. *Wendy Blake, Coventry College of Education.*

contact print on 'Kodalith' Ortho film to produce a high contrast negative.

(b) Then use an enlarger to produce a positive image of the final size required on a sheet of 'line' film. Develop with 'Kodalith' Super Developer powder, fix with 'Kodafix' solution. (Use a 25w safe lamp fitted in a Kodak safelight Filter No. 1A, when handling 'Kodalith' Ortho film.)

(c) Use nylon, terylene or silk on screen frame. After stretching degrease material by brushing it with 5% solution of caustic soda (wear gloves, avoid splashing on clothes, skin or in eyes).

(d) When dry, coat screen on inside with Seriset emulsion (Screen Process Supplies Ltd). Apply this with a piece of stiff card using a scraping action to obtain a thin, even layer. Then leave the screen to dry *in a dark-room*.

(e) After 2/3 hours screen is ready for exposure. Place the screen over a block of foam rubber, cut to fit just inside the frame. Then take the enlarged 'line' film positive image (b above) and place it with the emulsion side touching the outside of the screen. Hold it in contact with a sheet of clean, clear, glass.

With the film and screen thus held in uniform contact, expose the screen to daylight through the film by placing it near to a window for 15 to 30 minutes, depending on the brightness of the day.

(f) After exposure, remove the glass and the film and *immediately* soak the screen in water. Undeveloped parts will wash out leaving a negative design fired in the screen. Dry horizontally.

(g) Screen as usual. Clear up as dyestuff requires.

Silk screens can be used most effectively to print wallpaper with Pigment dyes or the Procion M range reactive dyes. Modern aerosol matt protective sprays may be used to obtain a surface resistant to wiping.

Plain coloured serviettes are also easily printed with Pigment dyes.

SUPPLIERS OF SILK SCREEN MATERIALS

Great Britain

Ashworth-Lyme Marquetry—114 Albion Road, New Mills, near Stockport.
Screen printing equipment including excellent frames, steamer, squeegees, etc.
S. Burrage Read & Co.—97 Blatchington Road, Hove, Sussex.
for Marvel 'Squeegeasy'.
Dryad Handicrafts—Northgates, Leicester.
George Hall (Sales) Ltd—St Thomas Place, Wellington Road, Stockport.
T. N. Lawrence & Son Ltd—24 Bleeding Heart Yard, Greville Street, London E.C.1.
Macclesfield Engineering Co. Ltd—Athey Street, Macclesfield, Cheshire.
E. T. Marler Ltd—14 Greville Street, Hatton Garden, London E.C.1.
Screen Process Supplies Ltd—24 Parsons Green Lane, London S.W.6.
Selectasine Silk Screens Ltd—22 Bulstrode Street, London W.1.
For Profilm, silk bolting cloth, screen sketching frames, etc.
Terylene Voile (ref. 3957 white) for covering screens—Alexander Jameson & Co. (Bonfab) Ltd, Bonfab Mills, Darvel, Ayrshire, Scotland.

USA

Art & Crafts Distributors Inc.—321 Park Avenue, Baltimore 1, Maryland.
Chicago Silk Screen Supply—882 Milwaukee Avenue, Chicago, Illinois.
Screen Process Supply Manufacturing Co.—1199E, 12th Street, Oakland, California.
Silk Screen Suppliers Inc.—32 Lafayette Avenue, New York, N.Y.
Standard Supply Co.—54 West 21st Street, New York, N.Y.

FURTHER SOURCES FOR MORE ADVANCED SCREEN PRINTING

Screen Printing by Taussig, Clayton Aniline Dye Co., Manchester, 1950.
Useful for historical information and technical details.

Although most of the following books refer to Screen printing on paper the ideas and techniques are often applicable to textiles.

Silk Screen Printing Production by J. I. Biegeleisen, Dover, N.Y., 1963.
Silk Screen Techniques by Biegeleisen and Cohn, Dover, N.Y., 1958.
A Guide to Screen Process Printing by F. Cain, Studio Vista, London, 1961.
Silk Screen Process Production by Hiett and Middleton, Blandford, London, 1960.
Simple Screen Printing by A. Kinsey, Leicester, 1968.
Introducing Screen Printing by A. Kinsey, Batsford, London, 1967.
The Art and Craft of Screen Process Printing by A. Kosloff, Bruce, N.Y., 1960.
Screen Printing on Fabric by V. Searle and R. Clayson, Studio Vista, London, 1968.
Print Making—a medium for basic design by P. Weaver, Studio Vista, 1968.
Although not specifically on screen printing this is an outstanding book for original thought and ideas upon the application of design.

NATURAL DYES: VEGETABLE AND MINERAL

MINERAL DYES

The first dyes used by primitive peoples were most probably water soluble. Mineral dyes were unknown in the ancient civilizations around the Mediterranean. Although powdered malachite was used as green eye shadow by the Egyptians in prehistoric times it is not known if attempts were made to colour cloth with ground rocks or iron rust apart from the method, that can hardly be called dyeing, of rubbing powdered pigment colours obtained from earths and minerals into the cloth with no further attempt to 'fix' the colour.

From the Middle Ages onwards until fairly recently, iron oxide dyes were used by certain East African tribes and around the Mediterranean, the sails of fishing boats and blinds were dyed deep reds with iron rust. In Europe, khaki fabrics for use in army equipment were produced with iron chrome pigments which were not only exceedingly fast to light and water but also rendered the fabric resistant to rotting and attack by insects and bacteria in humid climates. Iron pyrites have for long been known as a source of a dark brown/black dye. It and certain other 'false drugs' such as copper and iron filings were expressly forbidden in the reorganization of the French Dyeing Industry undertaken by Jean Baptiste Colbert towards the end of the seventeenth century.

Hand craftsmen, and particularly weavers, have long valued such mineral dyes as iron rust and manganese for producing relatively fast, strong colours. Apart from their staining quality that these and other minerals have in dyeing fabric, they have been used extensively in pigment dyestuffs. To hold the pigment to the fabric a number of natural binders, including albumen in particular, have been used. Recently great interest has been aroused by the availability of new forms of binders based on synthetic resins.

A dispersion of a coloured insoluble pigment together with a synthetic resin which is water soluble because it is used at an intermediate stage of its formation, is applied to the fabric and fixed after drying by a heat treatment for a few minutes at around 140°C. This completes the formation of the resin to make the pigment fast to light and washing. Recent improvements have reduced the tendency to stiffen the fabric and improved the fastness to wet rubbing although the 'handle' (feel) of a pigment printed fabric is usually appreciably stiffer than where 'true' dyestuffs have been employed.

103 Screen printed with vegetable dyes on a mordanted cloth. Steamed and washed. *Rita Martin, Coventry College of Education.*

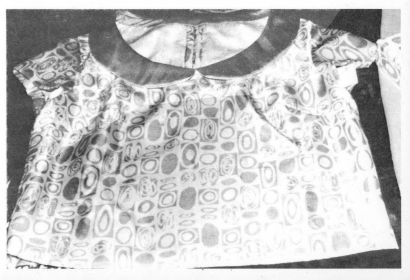

VEGETABLE DYES

The craft of vegetable dyeing is an ancient one, the earliest dyes being juices of fruits and berries, extracts of crushed flowers, roots and bark. It is likely that they were first used to colour the human body and later to decorate clothes and other fabrics. Pliny and other early writers describe in some detail the use of various substances such as Glastum or the woad plant, Indigo (blues); Kermes and Cochineal insects, Madder and Henna roots (all reds); purples from mussels found on parts of the Eastern Mediterranean and made in the smelly streets of Tyre; safflower (yellow); Saffron, an orange-yellow dye from the crocus flower and a black dye from Oak Galls. These are but a few of the dyes that have come down to us from antiquity.

There are three types of natural dye-stuffs:

1. Mordant dyes, e.g. weld, madder and cochineal.

These dyes have no direct affinity for wool but possess a great affinity for certain mineral salts or mordants which in turn have a great affinity for wool.

2. Substantive or non-mordant dyes, e.g. lichens, berberis (barberry), and elder. These dyes have a direct affinity for wool and need not be used with a mordant.

3. Vat dyes, e.g. indigo.

One of the few vat dyestuffs requiring little alkali which is a substance harmful to wool. The vat indigo produces a much more beautiful and permanent colour than indigo extract, but it is far more trouble to prepare and use.

There are four main mordants:

1. Alum—potash alum gives strong, clear colours but too much may make the wool sticky.

2. Chrome—bichromate of potash gives rich colours.

3. Iron-ferrous sulphate gives sad colours, but strong solutions harshen wool.

4. Tin—stannous chloride gives sharp colours, but too much may make wool brittle.

Many of these mordants will produce a different shade or colour from the same dye.

Fabrics need some preparation before use, partly to open the fibre and to make it more receptive to the dye and partly to remove impurities. Silk for instance has a waxy finish that needs to be removed by washing in warm, mild suds and rinsing well. Raw silk must also be stripped of its natural gum by 'de-gumming' for $1-1\frac{1}{2}$ hours in a solution containing 1 part olive oil soap per 100 parts of water at 95°C. The fabric is then rinsed well in water and dried. Wool is steeped in slightly soapy, hot water for ten minutes, wrung out and repeated in a new bath, then rinsed thoroughly in hot water. Very oily wool will need a temperature of 60°C. and further baths at 49°C. until the wool looks and smells clean, then it will need two or three rinses at 60°C. The wool must not be worked too vigorously nor subjected to sudden changes of temperature, or felting may occur. It should be evenly damp before entering the dyebath.

NOTE—Recipes for these dyes will be found on pages 128–134.

SUPPLIERS OF VEGETABLE & MINERAL DYES

In addition to the firms mentioned in the general lists of suppliers the following are recommended:

Great Britain

Vegetable dyestuffs are becoming very difficult to obtain but the following firms have been exceedingly co-operative.

Boots Pure Drug Co. Ltd—Head Office, Station Street, Nottingham.

Comak Chemicals Ltd—Swinton Works, Moon Street, London N.1.

L. A. Horner & Sons—9 Colworth Grove, Browning Street, London S.E.17.

British Drug Houses Ltd—Poole, Dorset.

Hopkins and Williams—Freshwater Road, Chadwell Heath, Essex.
(Particularly silver grain Cochineal and natural Indigo.)

Youngs of Leicester Ltd—40/42 Belvour Street, Leicester, (Youngs Fast Black).

Australia

D. Bailey—15 Dutton Street, Bankstown N.S.W.

Canada

Dominion Herb Distributors Inc.—136 Oneida Drive, Pointe Claire, Quebec, Canada.

FURTHER SOURCES FOR MORE ADVANCED WORK WITH VEGETABLE AND MINERAL DYES

Apart from the books mentioned in the General Bibliography the following are also recommended:

Lichens for Vegetable Dyeing by E. M. Bolton, Studio Vista, London, 1960.
An exhaustive book upon one aspect of natural dyes.

Dye Plants and Dyeing—Brooklyn Botanic Gardens, N.Y., 1964.
Covers the whole world and is full of ideas and recipes.

Using Wayside Plants by N. Coon, Hearthside Press Inc., N.Y., USA, 1960.

Yarn Dyeing by E. Davenport, Sylvan Press, London W.C.1, 1955.

The Dye Pot by M. F. Davidson, Shuttlecraft Shop, Middlesboro, Kentucky, 1950.

Natural Dyes by S. Hierstead, Bruce Humphries Inc., Boston, USA, 1950.
A good all-round book with useful recipes and tips.

Notes on Spinning and Dyeing Wool by M. Holding, Skilbeck Brothers Ltd, London S.E.15, 1922.

The Woad Plant and its Dye by J. B. Hurry, O.U.P., London.

Ancient and Medieval Dyes by W. F. Leggett, Chemical Publishing Co., N.Y., USA, 1944.
Includes a useful bibliography.

Vegetable Dyeing (E. Conley) revised by M. Lewis, Penland School of Handicrafts Inc., Penland, North Carolina, USA.

Vegetable Dyes by E. Mairet, Faber, London, 1939.
A most informative book by an experienced weaver and dyer.

Natural Organic Colouring Matters by Perkins and Everest, Longmans Green, London, 1918.
A standard work.

Processes in Dyeing with Vegetable Dye and other Means by F. Whipple Pope, North Bennet Street Industrial School, Boston 9, Mass., USA, 1960.
Particularly useful for North American plants.

The Use of Vegetable Dyes by V. Thurston, Dryad Press, Leicester, 1957.
A very useful book with good recipes and bibliography.

Navajo Native Dyes: their Preparation and Use by S. Young, (US Dept. of Interior), Haskell Institute, Lawrence, Kansas, USA, 1940.
Specialized but useful.

Natural Dyes in the United States by R. J. Adrosko, V. S. Gort, Printing office, Washington D.C., 1968.

DISCHARGE PRINTING

Certain dyes may be bleached with chemicals. This method is one of the most ancient known since it was first discovered that certain 'magic' streams would remove colour.

The fabric is first dyed an even colour and a chemical is applied either from a pad with vegetables, etc., or a block, or with a screen or in the tie-dye technique.

Simple experiments in this technique have already been described on page 69 and a list of dischargeable dyes follows this section. Certain of these dyestuffs are only dischargeable from pale or medium depths if white is required, alternatively a deep colour will only discharge to a medium tone and many dyes are not dischargeable at all.

The fabric is dyed an even colour in the appropriate manner for the dyestuff used. It is rinsed and dried in the usual way and then gummed down onto the printing surface. Then it is ready to be block or screen printed with the discharge paste.

Use it to print with, from a pad with potatoes, scraps, blocks or paint on with a brush or put through a screen. *Wherever and whatever it touches it will bleach to some extent so wear an overall and rubber gloves.*

Prints must not be left exposed to the air and should be dried as soon as possible after printing. This may be done with a portable convector heater or hair drier. As soon as possible the prints should be wrapped in *dry* cloths and steamed for five (thin material)—ten (thick material) minutes. After steaming, unwrap and rinse through at once. Steaming cloths and all bowls, blocks, screens, etc. should be washed out in cold water immediately after use. Recipes on pages 126 and 127.

Dylon Many Dylon multi-purpose dyes may be discharged to white or pale shades, Dygon may also be used, if desired, instead of Formosul for these dyes.

Procion (Reactive) The following Procion dyes will give even dischargeable ground shades on cotton, linen and viscose rayon.

Procion Brilliant Yellow	M-6GS	Procion Brilliant Red	H-7BS
Procion Brilliant Yellow	H-5GS	*Procion Brilliant Blue	H-7GS
Procion Brilliant Yellow	H-4GS	*Procion Brilliant Blue	H-5GS
*Procion Yellow	H-AS	*Procion Printing Green	H-B
*Procion Brilliant Orange	H-6RS	*Procion Printing Green	H-5G
*Procion Orange Brown	H-2GS	*Procion Black	H-GS
Procion Dark Brown	H-BS	*Procion Black	H-NS
*Will discharge to pale shades from deep			

Acid The following Acid dyes are suitable for dischargeable ground shades on wool and/or silk.

Carbolan Yellow	4GS	Coomassie Milling Scarlet	5BS
Carbolan Yellow	RS	Coomassie Red	PGS
Chrysophenine	GP	Coomassie Red	G125
Coomassie Yellow	RS	Ultralan Bordeaux	RS
Coomassie Milling Scarlet	GS	Ultralan Blue	2GS
Durazol Yellow	4GS	Chlorazol Orange	POP
Durazol Red	2BP	Chlorazol Orange Brown	X150
		Chlorazol Brown	BS
		Chlorazol Brown	MP

Direct The following Direct dyes are suitable for dischargeable ground shades on cotton, linen and viscose rayon.

Durazol Yellow	6GS	Durazol Blue	4RS
Durazol Flavine	RS	Durazol Grey	VGS
Durazol Orange	RS	Durazol Grey	BS
Durazol Brown	BRS	Chlorazol Fast Pink	BKS
Durazol Green	4G	Chlorazol Fast Helio	2RKS
Durazol Brilliant Red	BS	Chlorazol Fast Red	FS
Durazol Helio	BS	Chlorazol Black	ES
Durazol Violet	B	Chlorazol Black	GFS
Durazol Blue	GS		

104 Cloth printed by the Discharge method. Cloth originally dyed dark brown/black by soaking in a dye made from bark and leaves. Design painted on in mud which probably contains iron acetate and then repainted over with a local soap containing potash to act as a mordant. A final repaint with mud is allowed to dry in the sun. The dye is bleached out to show red-brown on a very dark ground. Bambara tribe, French Sudan. *Courtesy Musée de l'Homme, Paris.*

105 Screen printed discharge in Formosul on a cloth dyed with Chlorazol Black E200 and then steamed and washed. *Wendy Blake, Coventry College of Education.*

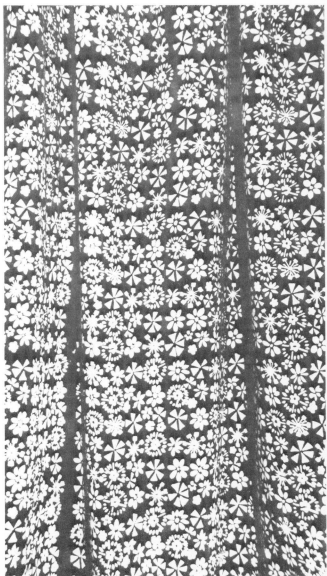

DESIGNING

The basic techniques of many forms of textile decoration have been described in the previous pages. Further sections give the recipes for many different dyestuffs. But both these ingredients are only of use if they are linked by an appropriate form of design.

With each particular technique it is important that the design exploits the particular qualities of the tools, methods and fabric used. In addition, the design must be considered in relation to the type, weight and final use of the fabric. The fabric may be required to lie flat (table mats and cloths), to be draped and folded (scarves, clothes, curtains), to be stretched (upholstery) or to be hung and stretched (hangings and collage). A design suitable for fine silk will rarely suit wool, linen, cotton, synthetics or even heavy silk.

In designing, much can be achieved by taking simple materials and allowing them to dictate the pattern. As already described in the section on screen printing, cut or torn greaseproof paper will give excellent screen designs (see page 94).

Ideas can be helped by building up a collection of source references. Illustrations can often be found in magazines, sales and travel literature, photographs, labels, fabric samples, etc. Sketch books may be kept to note colours and shapes with mounted examples of different hues, tones, shades and textures of each colour.

Sources available to designers may be conveniently divided under four main headings. The following lists are only a beginning. A good designer tries to cultivate both an alert eye and an enquiring mind able to see unusual views and combinations.

Historical sources (Figure 106):
Alphabets (particularly Chinese, Japanese, Turkish and other Oriental examples). Manuscript illuminations, Egyptian hieroglyphs and tablet markings. Pottery decoration (especially Chinese, Japanese, Greek and Central American). Textile decoration (such as Indian tie and dye, Javanese batik, Oriental rugs and embroidery), African carvings. American Indian decoration on wigwams, blankets, hides and totem poles. Oceanic weapons, canoes, houses, dinkira and tapa cloths and other patterns. Architectural shapes and decorations, especially Russian, Byzantine, Chinese, Indian, Japanese and Central American. Mexican pre-conquest Magic books. Heraldic devices. Cave paintings. Chinese, Polish and Vietnam paper cuts. Brass rubbings. Chinese tomb rubbings. Engravings on Anglo-Saxon and other jewellery. Carvings on early boxes and chests. Victorian fans, valentines, cards, lace, crochet, combs. Weapons (particularly Oriental ones). Pargetting. Stage coach shapes (wheels, brasses, shape). Mosaics. Boat shapes. Early machines (balloons, aeroplanes, bicycles, trains, looms, spinning wheels).

Natural sources (Figures 107 and 108):
Plants, leaves, grasses, flowers, mosses, fern, cacti, trees, branches, twigs, fruits, vegetables, rock formations, tree sections. Seed heads, cobwebs, feathers, fossils, shells, seaweed, leaf and fish skeletons, birds' eggs, frost patterns, fingerprints. Animals, insects, reptiles, caterpillars, tropical fish, sea creatures and plants, marine animals, wings. Bark rubbings, wood graining, rock markings, marble, snake skin, crystalline and precious or semi-precious stone surfaces, ground surfaces, seashore markings, wave shapes, magnetic fields, oil marks on wet roads, detergent foam.

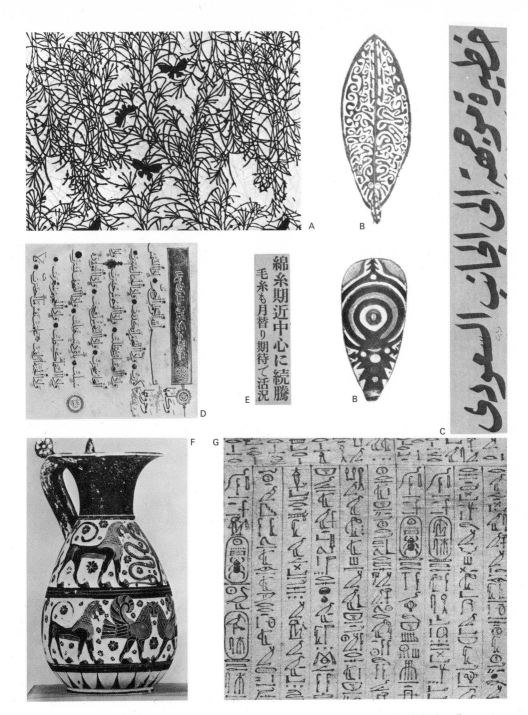

106   A.   Old Japanese stencil held together by human hairs. *Courtesy H. Steiner Esq.*
         B.   Polynesian shields. *Courtesy Grant Collection, Boston, Mass.*
         C.   Arabic writing.
         D.   Koran, Arabic MS, Egypt, fourteenth century. *Courtesy British Museum.*
         E.   Japanese writing.
         F.   Corinthian Wine Jug 625–600 B.C. *Courtesy British Museum.*
         G.   Detail of a Hieroglyphic Text, Egyptian *c.* 1450 B.C. *Courtesy Museum of Fine Arts, Boston, Mass.*

107   A.   Poppy Seed cases cut open.   E.   Wood grain on a piece of veneer.
        B.   Leaf of cardinal climber.   F.   Dandelion clock.
        C.   Tulip tree leaf.   G.   Ripples on a pond.
        D.   Seed head of wild carrot.   H.   Desiccated leaf.
(Photographs courtesy Robert Armstrong collection)

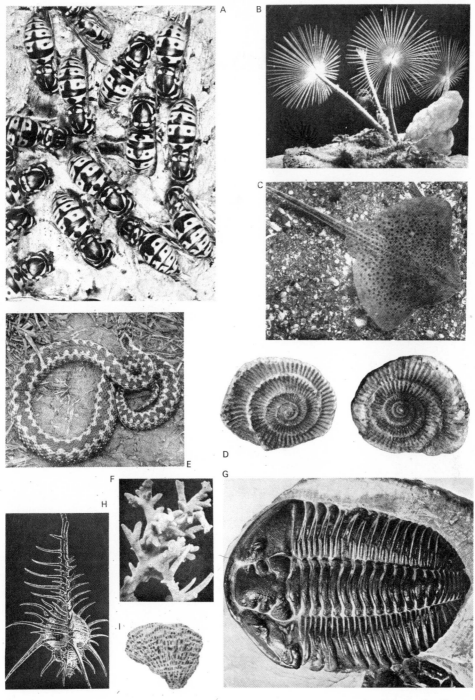

108   A. Wasps.   D. Ammonite fossil.   G. Tribolite fossil.
        B. Peacock worms.   E. Adder or viper.   H. Sea shell.
        C. Ray fish.   F. Stag's Horn coral.   I. Coral.

(Photographs courtesy Robert Armstrong collection)

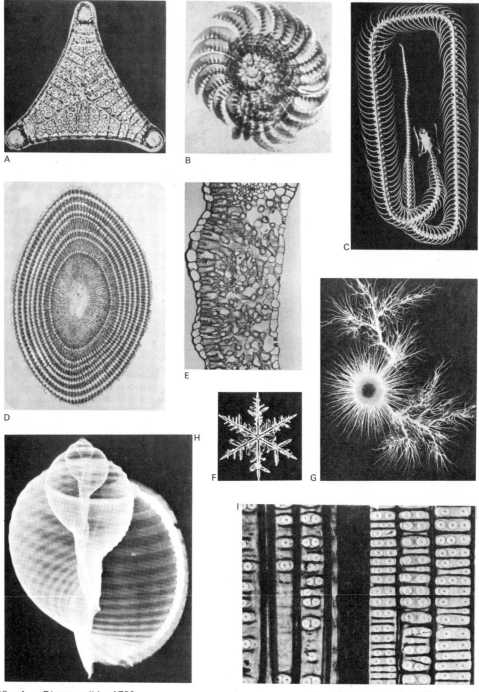

109 A. Diatom cell by 1700.
   B. Polystomella, empty shells of minute organisms by 150.
   C. Skeleton of a snake.
   D. Cross section of a sea urchin's spine by 300.
   E. Section of a leaf by 100.
   F. Snow crystal by 1500.
   G. Electrical discharge.
   H. X-ray photograph of a shell.
   I. Radial section of redwood by 700

(Photographs courtesy Robert Armstrong collection)

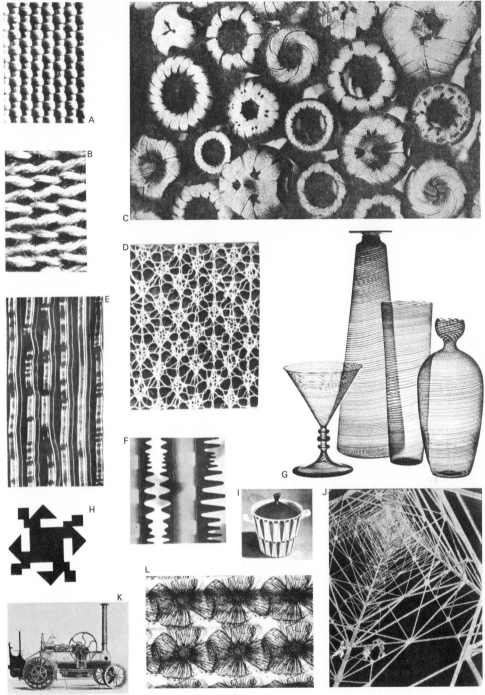

110 A. Plain woven fabric.
       B. Plain knitted fabric.
       C. Diamond coring and drill bits made by
           Christiansens Diamond Products.
       D. Loose string construction.
    E and F Highly magnified grooves in a
          gramophone record.

G. Unusual contemporary shapes.
H. Contemporary trade mark.
I. Contemporary container.
J. Erecting a 415 feet high tower.
K. Steam Traction Engine of *c.* 1870. *Photograph
     courtesy J. Redgrave.*
L. Contemporary fabric.

A B

C D

111 A. Angel Pavement designed by Pat Albeck for the Young Sanderson 1969 Collection. 48 in. wide version of a peasant border stripe. *Courtesy Sanderson Fabrics.*

B. Tornrosa, a screen print designed by Viola Grasten for Mölnlycke Hemtexil, Sweden.

C. Alhambra designed by Mary Yonge for Edinburgh weavers. 24 in. repeat based on Moorish tiles and intended for curtains or covers. *Courtesy Edinburgh weavers.*

D. Reciprocation designed by Barbara Brown for Heals Fabrics, 48 in. wide machine screen print on crêpe cotton with approximate 30 in. repeat. *Courtesy Heals Fabrics Ltd.*

Microscopic sources (Figure 109):
Molecular structure, diatoms, cross sections, cells, snowflakes, textile fibres.

Other sources (Figure 110):
Intricate man-made objects (watches, cast and wrought iron, musical instruments, sewing machines). Aerial photographs. Blue prints. Architects' drawings. Trade Marks. Modern abstract painting, construction and sculpture. Mathematical shapes. Fireworks. Blots. Computer cards. Geometrical shapes. Tool shapes. Road signs. Spirograph designs. Springs. Lines on wet blotting or cartridge paper. Contour lines, star galaxies, marbled papers, armour, kaleidoscopes. Glassware shapes.

It is important to ensure that where a design has to be worked out before printing, the unit used should fit into the width of fabric. The most usual size for furnishing fabrics is 48 to 50 in. and for dress fabrics 36 in. Certain cotton fabrics (intended originally for the manufacture of sheets and pillow cases) are often supplied in a wide variety of widths from 18 to 90 in. Silk is also supplied in 30 and 48-in. widths. Pieces of fabric can vary from 30 to 120 yards depending on the weight of the fabric.

When planning an all-over pattern it will often save a great deal of time to prepare sixteen identical units, cutting out each unit and then experimenting with varying arrangements of drops, shifts, inverted stripes, etc., to see the joining of the pattern in different positions.

A small floodlight or large torch with coloured gelatines will help to show the effect of a pattern on different coloured grounds. An alternative is to look at the design on white paper through pieces of tinted sweet wrapping cellophane or lighting gelatines.

It is also sometimes useful to look at the reflection of a design in a mirror. The unusual view will often show up weaknesses in the basic design.

When the design is finally agreed it is still important not to look upon the chosen method as merely a way of copying the painted or drawn design onto the fabric. The method should alter the design to fit its own limitations and the designer should be prepared to adapt the design as it is printed.

Many designers do not design in colour but work in black, shades of grey and white on a medium grey paper. This allows the design to be translated at a later date into colours with similar tones.

Film and transparencies may be used as a source of inspiration. *NON*-inflammable film will blister when a match flame or glowing piece of string is put near to the film or transparency. When viewed or projected the abstract pattern is a most inspiring source of pattern. A further development is to put two or more 'burnt' transparencies together in one mount, or to combine an unburnt and burnt together, or two unburnt together or pieces of coloured cellophane (sweet wrappings). Waterproof markers may be used on the film to blot out parts, add colours, texture etc.

Other suggestions can include the trapping, between two pieces of thin plastic, of threads, seeds, ground pigments and the like. These are then projected. Edges may be bound with sellotape.

Alternatively one piece of self-adhesive film and one piece of thin plastic may be used.

Spots of oil, colour water, coloured ink, etc. may be placed between the pieces of thin plastic before edges are sealed. The heat of the projector lamps will cause the trapped liquids to change patterns.

GENERAL SOURCES

On Designing by A. Albers, Pellango Press. Mainly woven textiles.

Elements of Design by D. Anderson, Holt Reinhart, London, 1961.
Historical approach to the subject.

Design—Sources and Resources by Ballinger and Vroman, Studio Vista, London, 1965.
Exceedingly useful with many excellent illustrations.

Design for You by Beitler and Lockhart, John Wiley, London, 1965.
Good sources and application.

Decorative Art of Egypt and Asia:
Folk Art of Primitive Peoples:
Folk Art of Europe all by H. Th. Bossert, Zwemmer, London, 1956.
Outstandingly useful to the designer, each volume contains many hundreds of coloured examples of primitive and folk art.

Design on Fabrics by Johnston, Meda, Parker and Kaufman, Reinhold, N.Y., 1967.

Eye for Colour by Bernat Klein, Collins, London, 1965.

Designs for Craftsmen by W. Miles, Doubleday, USA, (Bell & Co., London), 1962.
Exceedingly well illustrated and useful with many sources illustrated.

Design by Accident by J. F. O'Brien, Dover Publications, N.Y., 1968.

Creative Paper Craft by E. Rottger, Batsford, London.
Many ideas appropriate to textile design. An outstanding book.

Teaching Design and Form by G. Sneum, Batsford, London, 1965.
Full of ideas and sources for the designer.

HISTORICAL SOURCES

Ancient Arts of the Andes by Bennett, Museum of Modern Art, N.Y., USA.

Art and Life in Ancient Mexico by C. Burland, Cassirrer, Oxford, 1953.

Magic Books from Mexico by C. Burland, King Penguin No. 64, 1953.

Prehistoric Cave Painting by R. Cuvey, Methuen, 'Movements in World Art Series', London, 1963.
One of several series from this publisher of well-illustrated small monographs on various aspects of art, containing useful material for the designer.

Egyptian Paintings by Davies, King Penguin No. 71, 1954.

Design Motifs of Ancient Mexico by J. Encisco, Constable, London, 1947.

The Written Word by Etiemble, Prentice Hall, London, 1961.
One of a very good series of books full of ideas.

Manual of Historic Ornament by Glazier, Batsford, London.

Art of the World: India by Goetz, Methuen, London.
One of a useful series.

Wycinanka Ludowa by Josef Grabowski, Wydawnnictno Sztuka, Warsaw, 1955.
Text in Polish, many illustrations of Polish paper cuts.

Treasures of the British Museum by G. Grigson, Thames & Hudson, London.

Costume Cavalcade by H. Hansen, Methuen, London, 1956.

Chinese Paper Cutouts by J. Hezlar, Spring Books, London, 1960.

Ceramic Art of China by W. B. Honey, Faber, London.

The Book of Signs by R. Koch, Dover (Constable), 1930.

Chinese Paper Cut Pictures by N. Kuo, Tiranti, London, 1964.

Art of the World: Africa by Leuzinger, Methuen, London.

26 Letters by O. Ogg, Harrap, London, 1955.

Laternenbilder aus China by A. Sailer, Buckheim Verlag Feldafurg Obb, 1955. Text in German, booklet on Chinese paper cuts.

Folk Art in Pictures—Tiranti, London.

Masks of West Africa by L. Underwood, Tiranti, London, 1964.

MICRO PHOTOGRAPHIC SOURCES

Snow Crystals by W. A. Bentley and W. J. Humphreys, Dover, N.Y., 1962.

The Universe by D. Bergamini, Time-Life International, N.Y., 1964.

The Living Rocks by S. Célébonovic, Phoenix House, London, N.D. Some most interesting detailed photographs of rock formations.

The Microstructure of Cells by S. W. Hurry, Murray, London, 1965.

Life Under the Microscope by Jirovec, Boucek and Fiala, Spring Books, London, 1959. Outstanding photographs useful for design.

The Thirteen Steps to the Atom by C. N. Martin, Harrap, London.

The Cell by John Pfeiffer, Time-Life International, 1965.

Plant Marvels in Miniature by C. Postma, Harrap, London, 1960.

Photomicrographs of the Flowering Plant by Shaw, Lazell & Foster, Longmans, London, 1965.

Forms and Patterns in Nature by W. Strache, Peter Owen, London, 1959.

Formen Des Mikrokosmos by C. Strüwe, Prestel-Verlag, Munchen (F. Lewis, Leigh on Sea).

Pattern and Texture by D. Wedd, Studio, London, 1956.

NATURAL SOURCES

Naturen som formgivare by B. Bager, Nordisk Rotogravyr, Stockholm, Sweden, 1961. Text in Swedish, excellent photos of dried seed heads, etc. English edition available.

The Open Sea by A. Hardy, Collins, London.

Handbook of Floral Ornament by R. G. Hatton, Dover, N.Y., 1960.

Plants that Feed Us and *Plants that Serve Us* both by E. Hvass, Blandford, London, 1960.

The Wonders of Wild Life in Europe by Roedelberger and Groschoff, Constable, London, 1963.

Trees and Bushes in Wood and Hedgerow by Vedel and Lange, Methuen, London, 1960. Excellent diagrams and illustrations for the designer.

Tropical Aquarium Fish in Colour by G. Vevers, Witherby, London, 1957.

The Sea Shore by C. Yonge, Collins, London.

OTHER SOURCES

Picasso by Elgar and Maillard, Thames & Hudson, London.

Abstract Art by F. Gore, Methuen, London, 1956.

Designing Tapestry by Lurçat, Rockliff.

Dictionary of Abstract Painting by M. Seuphar, Methuen, London.

Microscope slides of diatoms, sections, etc., are obtainable from A. Clarkson, 338 High Holborn, London E.C.1.

Transparencies which represent sources of inspiration and which include close-up details of plants, trees, seed heads, animals, etc., X-ray photographs of shells, fishes, etc., rock and mineral formations, etc., are made by and obtainable from Dr Block Color Productions, 1309, North Genesee Avenue, Hollywood 46, California, USA. Also obtainable in Great Britain from The Miniature Gallery, 60 Rushett Close, Long Ditton, Surrey.

The *Looking and Seeing* Filmstrips, 81 Southway, London N.20, also cover design and includes a variety of source material.

112 'Vanity', a resist and painted wall hanging by Michael O'Connell. After studying primitive art in Africa, the Antipodes and the Pacific he specialized for many years with china clay as a resist medium and dyes fixed by oxidization. His many large hangings and murals have been shown and purchased throughout the world. He now lives and works at Perry Green, Much Hadham, Hertfordshire.

113 Screen printed hanging with machine embroidered decoration and appliquéd areas by Romaine Pattinson— *Coventry College of Education*.

114　Direct dyed, tie and dyed on cotton. Bands of running stitches, of oversewing stitches and running stitches on double cloth for the diamonds. *Courtesy Anne Maile. Photograph Chris Asford.*

115   Vat dyed, tie and dyed on cotton. Large, medium and small stones tied in cloth with binding thread added over the stones. *Courtesy Anne Maile. Photograph Chris Asford*

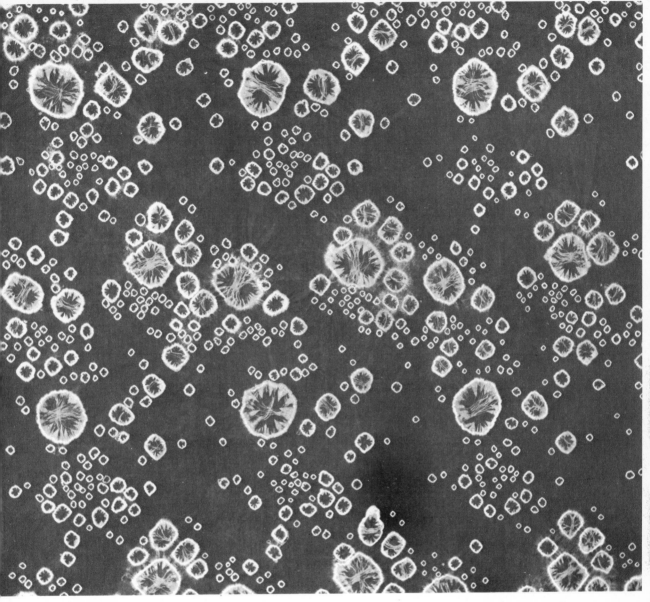

117 Vat dyed, tie and dyed on cottons. Stones tied in the cloth to form a repeat pattern. *Courtesy Anne Maile.*
Photograph Chris Asford.

116 Three screen printed hangings. These are first exercises printed with Polyprint pigment dyes through screens blocked out, with paper or wax. They are built up without preliminary drawings and directly with the screen upon the fabric. *Coventry College of Education.*

118 Long, narrow, halter-necked dress in African cotton and screen printed in white, navy and yellow, with a long motif of enormous eyes. *By Veronica Marsh. Photograph after Helmut Newton.*

119 Screen printed hanging. Printed with Cibacron reactive dyes by the catalyst method, 3 by 7 ft. *By Elizabeth Tate—Coventry College of Education.*

RECICES

GENERAL NOTES

1. The addition of a few drops of methylated spirits will often help to dissolve an obstinate dye powder when pasting it in a little water prior to adding it to the dyebath.

2. An acid gum can be neutralized with a few drops of ammonia stirred into the thickening.

3. Small sample pieces printed or dyed in the same manner and with the recipe to be used for the actual printing should not be wasted. They can be made up into a great variety of small objects such as egg cosies, needle cases, pin cushions, book marks, glass and other small mats, comb cases, cosmetic bags (plastic lined), serviette rings and dolls' clothes.

4. Larger samples still can be made up into beach bags, hats, bags, night wear cases, ties, serviettes, cushion covers, and scarves.

5. Full pieces may be used to make table cloths, curtains, hangings and clothes.

6. Wet colours always appear darker and deeper than when dry. Before throwing away a dyebath check correct colour by squeezing out the fabric and ironing a corner at correct fabric temperature to see final colour.

7. Soft water gives the best results with most dyes.

8. Rinsing is very important to get rid of all surplus dye, alkali, acid or chemicals.

9. Ball point and plunger containers when emptied should be washed out and used to draw lines. As long as the dye used is thin enough to flow evenly, the results are excellent. Such containers as Platignum Spot-Stick. Roll-on deodorants and 'Casual' hair tinting applicators (Smiths plastic containers) are all good and much easier to control than brushes.

ACID DYES

Are suitable for natural silk and chlorinated wool (special recipes are required for certain acid dyes on a number of synthetic fibres including viscose rayon, nylon, orlon and terylene). Although this group contains a large number of dyes which differ in their basic chemical structure they have one feature in common. This is that they are all suitable for application to the above fibres in an acid dyebath.

The dyebath contains Glauber's salt which helps dissolve the dye and, by restraining its entry into the fibres, evens out the dye absorption by the fabric. A later addition of a small amount of acetic or diluted sulphuric acid corrects the restraint of the salt and helps to exhaust the dyebath.

Acid dyes are easy to apply and many are fast, bright colours. In the main they have little affinity with cellulose or acetate fibres. Certain colours are dischargeable. They are excellent for tie and dye work.

RECIPES

The following methods will be found satisfactory for most acid dyes of reasonable fastness. For more detailed recipes refer to *An Introduction to Textile Printing* published by Butterworth & Co.

Piece and Tie Dyeing

(a) $\frac{1}{2}$–1 level teaspoon of dye thoroughly pasted in a little cold water in a large bowl.

(b) 1 pint of boiling water is poured onto this dye paste, stirring until it is completely dissolved. If necessary, boil and strain.

(c) Place the fabric as open as possible in an empty dyebath. Pour on sufficient warm water to cover the fabric during the dyeing (see note 3). Remove the fabric squeezing surplus water back into the dyebath. Add the prepared dye liquor to water in the dyebath, and stir. Then add

(d) 1–2 level tablespoons of Glauber's salt dissolved in a little warm water, and
(e) 1–2 level teaspoons of acetic acid and stir.
(f) Immerse the evenly damp fabric in the bath and dye for about 1 hour (in piece dyeing at, but not above 95°C., 205°F.), keeping the fabric in as open a width as possible and gently moving it with clean smooth stirring rods (see note 4).
(g) After dyeing, rinse and dry as open as possible.
(h) Clean up with a warm water/detergent solution.

Screen Printing

(a) 1 level teaspoon (pale)–5 level teaspoons (deep) of dye is pasted with
(b) 5–10 teaspoons of glycerine and added to
(c) $\frac{1}{3}$ pint of hot water.
Boil and strain the mixture if necessary until the colour is completely dissolved and then stir into
(d) 1 pint prepared Manutex (GB), Keltex (USA) or Nafka thickening, leave to cool (see note 1).
(e) When cold add **either**:
  1. 5 level teaspoons of tartaric acid dissolved in 5 level teaspoons of water **or**
  2. 5 level teaspoons of Perminal KB
     5 level teaspoons of Ammonium Oxalate dissolved in
     15 level teaspoons of hot water.
(f) Print, then dry and steam for 1 hour.
(g) After fixing, rinse thoroughly in cold water, then wash carefully in a warm Lissapol ND, Stergene, Teepol (GB); Synthrapol or Duponal (USA) solution ($\frac{1}{2}$ level teaspoon–1 quart of water). Rinse in cold water. Iron on reverse whilst still damp.

Block and Pad Printing
Reduce the amount of thickening used in the above recipe by $\frac{1}{2}$ or as required.

Direct Painting
Reduce the amount of thickening by $\frac{3}{4}$ or until the mixed dyestuff flows easily.

NOTES
1. Manutex F may be used as a thickener in place of Nafka, in which case reduce the hot water (d) to $\frac{3}{4}$ pint and use the Perminal KB etc., of (e)2.
2. NEVER leave wet fabrics about in piles, ALWAYS rinse as quickly as possible after fixing and hang out in open width until dry.
3. The amount of water (preferably soft) used in a dyebath should be at least 30/40 times the weight of the dry fabric. For tie dyeing, calculate the weight on the amount of untied dry fabric.
4. Tie dyes may be dropped in and taken out of the dyebath at any time—from a few seconds to ten minutes as required colour is reached. But this may not give optimum dye fastness which requires full dyeing time.
5. Rinse tie-dye after dyeing and partially dry before untying.

DIRECT DYES
Are suitable for cotton, linen, and viscose rayon. Some are also suitable for silk and wool. These dyes are soluble in water and will dye without the use of a mordant. The presence in the dyebath of common salt or Glauber's salt helps in the absorption of the dye by the cellulose fibre.

All tend to give level dyeing and many are of the 'Azo' type which are fairly easily discharged or bleached out to the original fabric colour without adversely affecting the fibre.

This class of man-made dyes is exceedingly large and can be intermixed but care must be taken to select ones of suitable fastness to light and washing as direct dyes vary greatly in this respect.

They are easy to apply and particularly suitable for tie and dye work.

RECIPES

Suitable for cotton, linen, viscose rayon, as well as some suitable for silk and wool.

Piece and tie dyeing on cotton, linen and viscose rayon.

(a) $\frac{1}{2}$-1 (or more for deep tones) level teaspoon of dye thoroughly pasted in a little cold water in a saucepan.

Add

(b) $\frac{1}{2}$ pint of boiling water, boil until dissolved.

(c) Place the fabric, as open as possible, in an empty dyebath. Pour on sufficient warm water to cover the fabric during the dyeing (see note 1). Remove the fabric, squeezing surplus water back into the dyebath. Add to water in the dyebath, the prepared dye liquor and stir.

(d) Immerse the wet fabric in the bath and slowly heat the dyebath up to 95°C. (205°F.) (i.e. just below boiling point.) Gently move the submerged fabric (in as open a width as possible for piece dyeing).

(e) Add slowly 10% (for pale shades)– 40% (for deep shades) Glauber's salt (or common salt) calculated on the weight of the dry fabric. This should be added in four equal portions at five-minute intervals whilst the temperature of the dyebath is maintained at just below boiling for $\frac{3}{4}$-1 hour or until most of the colour has gone from the water, i.e. the dyebath has been 'exhausted'. Continue to work the fabric well during dyeing to obtain an even shade on the fabric.

(f) After dyeing, rinse and dry as open as possible.

(g) Clean up with a warm water/detergent solution.

NOTES

1. The amount of water (preferably soft) used in a dyebath should be at least 30/40 times the weight of the dry fabric. For tie dyeing calculate weight on the amount of untied dry fabric.

2. When using these dyes on silk, use common salt instead of Glauber's. Never allow the dyebath to boil as boiling will de-lustre the silk. For wool 1 level teaspoon of acetic acid may be added to the dyebath at the beginning and again near the end of the dyeing. Do not stir wool too vigorously or it may felt.

3. NEVER leave the wet fabrics about in piles, ALWAYS rinse as quickly as possible after fixing and hang out in open width until dry.

Screen printing for cotton, linen and viscose rayon.

(a) 1 level teaspoon (pale)–5 level teaspoons (deep) of dye pasted with

(b) 4 level teaspoons of urea (note 2) in a little hot water and add

(c) $\frac{1}{3}$ pint of boiling water and boil until dissolved, then strain the mixture through a fine mesh into the prepared thickening (Manutex, Keltex or Nafka). Stir in a little at a time until the required depth of colour is obtained (note 1). When cold add

(d) $1\frac{1}{2}$ level teaspoons of disodium hydrogen phosphate which has been dissolved in a *little* warm water.

(e) Print, then dry and steam for 1 hour. This can be shortened to 30/45 minutes if a star steamer is used.

(f) After fixing, rinse thoroughly in cold water and then wash carefully in a warm Lissapol ND, Stergene, Teepol (GB); Synthropol or Duponal (USA) solution ($\frac{1}{2}$ level teaspoon–1 quart of warm water). Rinse in cold water. Iron on the reverse while still damp.

GENERAL NOTES

1. If the finished dye is too thick, add a little cold water to thin it. If too thin add a little of the thicker gum.

2. If parts of the dye are increased up to six then increase the urea pro rata but only have sufficient boiling water to dissolve the dye.

Urea is used to dissolve and spread the dyestuff evenly during a steaming. The quantity required needs adjusting to the local steaming conditions. Inspect the test pieces very carefully for 'spreading', 'bleeding', 'marking-off', 'fading' and any other faults before commencing on the lengths.

Bleeding can be reduced in moist steaming conditions by using less urea, but do test the pieces first and wash thoroughly. (Also see note 5.)

3. If difficulties are experienced in obtaining an even take-up of the printing paste by the fabric an addition of 2% of Perminal KB to the printing paste is advised.

4. Excessive bleeding during washing off may be improved by a rinse in a Fixanol PN bath. This is generally prepared by adding 1 part Fixanol PN into 1000 parts of cold rinsing water. After washing off in Fixanol PN the fabric should be dried *immediately* without further rinsing, then ironed on the reverse as usual.

5. NEVER leave wet fabrics about in piles. ALWAYS rinse as quickly as possible and hang out to dry in open width until ironing on reverse.

Block and pad printing

Reduce the amount of thickener by half or as necessary.

Direct painting

Reduce the amount of thickener by three-quarters or as necessary to flow from the brush.

DISCHARGE PRINTING
Formosul

Formosul CW and Redusol Z are similar substances to Formosul but contain whitening agents to give a whiter discharge on wool and silk.

RECIPE

Use prepared Manutex (GB) or Keltex (USA) gum and mix to the consistency of the required printing paste.

Put 9 parts of this prepared thickening and 1 part of Formosul into a saucepan. Stir slowly over gentle heat until dissolved. If necessary, neutralize with a little ($\frac{1}{80}$ part) Tetrasodium Pyrophosphate.

N.B.: If a strong colour is to be discharged, 2 parts Formosul may be used. Basically simple to use, great care must be taken to keep Formosul dry, and these rules should be followed:

(a) Dry the cloths and newspapers for steaming before starting to print, as these must be thoroughly dry. Have fabric gummed down onto printing surface.

(b) *Open Formosul container only when ready to use.*

(c) *Close immediately after use, to prevent Formosul absorbing moisture from the atmosphere.*

(d) As mixed Formosul is transparent, make sure there is none on the fingers before printing a block or screen.

(e) Use a convector heater and dry the fabric as soon as possible after printing and whilst on the table (an alternative is a portable hair drier).

(f) Formosul should be printed, dried, steamed and washed in one day; it must *not* be left overnight before steaming.

(g) Mix only enough for immediate use, as it will not keep overnight.

(h) The steamer must be packed as quickly as possible and left on full for the duration of the steaming.

(i) Short steam (5–10 minutes), according to the thickness of material and the depth of colour being discharged. Silk should only require five minutes. Heavy linen *may* need ten minutes but never longer.

(j) Wash the fabric *very* thoroughly, also brush, table, felt, pad, and/or screen and squeegee as soon as possible after completion.

(k) Formosul CW and Redusol Z give a chalkier white, but they are mixed and used in the same way.

GENERAL NOTES

1. Formosul has a very strong, unpleasant smell and should be stored in the dry, in securely closed containers.
2. Small areas of Formosul printed fabric may be discharged by drying with a heater and ironing with a steam iron or pressing with a damp cloth.
3. Take care, as odd drops of discharge will bleach almost any colour to some extent. Wear an overall of some kind.
4. Since discharge agents are able to destroy some dyes but not others it is possible to mix a non-dischargeable dye with the discharge (using the correct dye recipe but with only sufficient thickening required for the particular printing process to be used). When correctly processed the discharge will remove the background colour but leave the non-dischargeable dye colour in its place. This method is employed extensively in commercial printing. Further methods include printing in a non-dischargeable dye on a dischargeable ground colour and then part overprinting with a discharge or a discharge containing a non-dischargeable dye. It need not be added that many experiments and much patience are essential if success is to be obtained.

DYLON

Multi-purpose dyes in forty-seven colours. Very useful for schools but not as fast as some other classes of dyestuffs.

Suitable for most synthetic and all natural fibres.

Available in two forms: (1) as a powder in small aluminium tins containing 5–8 grams of dye from local retailers or in 500-gram (1 lb.) tins from the manufacturers; (2) as a liquid in a restricted range of colours packed in plastic bottles containing $4\frac{1}{4}$ fluid ozs of dye and salt. Supplied by local stockists. Full recipes are given with each small tin.

DYLON COLD WATER DYES

There are six pale and twelve deep colours all developed from Procion dyes.

Suitable for cotton, linen, viscose rayon, silk and wool (not cashmere, angora and mohair).

Available in small aluminium tins containing 10 grams of dye from local retailers. In 4-oz. and 1-lb.-tins from the manufacturers. Again full recipes are given with each small tin.

NOTE: When washing cold water dyed fabrics avoid the use of chlorine-type bleaches.

GENERAL NOTES

1. A whole tin of dye need not be used at one time, either use half the powder or liquid dye and half the above chemicals and water or mix dye separately from alkaline solution and then mix these together in equal parts as needed.
2. Other Dylon dyes include Wash'n Dye for use in washing machines (all the above dyes may also be used in machines), carpet dyes, Dygon (a bleach), a special Black, nylon whiteners, etc.

NATURAL DYES—MINERAL
Iron rust 1

Contains highly poisonous substances and must only be used by responsible persons and the ingredients kept under lock and key.

Gives a tan brown on cottons and linen.

Requirements
Plastic dyebath such as a large bucket or dustbin (keep this container for iron use only), smooth stirring rods, spoons, rag, rubber gloves, heating ring and hanging facilities. Ferrous sulphate, lead acetate (**poison**) caustic soda, soap, hot and cold water.

Method
(a) Place 1 gallon of hot water in a container and pour in 1 lb. of ferrous sulphate. Stir until thoroughly dissolved.

(b) Pour into (a) $\frac{1}{2}$ lb. of lead acetate, stir thoroughly and leave for several hours before use.

(c) Pour, syphon or strain off the iron liquor into the dyebath without disturbing the sediment. *This sediment must be thrown away immediately the liquor has been taken off.* Clean the container at once before the sediment sets hard.

(d) Prepare the fabric by squeezing in a solution of detergent and cold water.

(e) Immerse the evenly damp fabric in the cold rust bath for one hour, turning periodically. Lift out, squeeze lightly and dry.

Run marks may be prevented by immediate fixing (as f) before drying the fabric.

(f) Fix by immersing the dyed fabric in a caustic soda bath ($\frac{1}{2}$ lb. caustic soda flakes stirred into 4 gallons of cold water) for two minutes and hang out to oxidize.

(g) When dry, finish with a rinse in cold water followed by a hot soapy water bath and plenty of warm rinsing.

GENERAL NOTES
1. This gives a strong colour. For a paler shade leave in the dye for a shorter time.

2. Very strong colour stiffens the fabric.

3. Lead acetate is necessary for printing recipes. If dyeing is done without lead a paler shade is obtained.

4. For printing by block or screen, reduce the amount of hot water in (a) to 1 quart, leave for 2 hours, decant, throw away the sediment at once and mix equal parts of this liquor with British Gum prepared very thick (1 part gum–1 part cold water, mixed to a paste, heated in a double saucepan and stirred until clear and dark. Half pint of hot water is added and stirred well. It is then ready for use.) Print and leave until dry. Fix as for dyeing.

5. A similar mixture of rust liquor and gum may be adjusted for direct brush painting with hot water. It may also be used over a flour paste resist or over wax in batik work.

Iron rust 2
To give a black on cottons and linen.

Method
(a) Gall the fabric as described on page 134 leaving it completely submerged in the galling bath overnight.

(b) Remove from the bath, squeeze out and open out to dry without rinsing. Do not allow it to touch the iron whilst wet or black marks will appear. Iron when dry.

(c) Prepare the dye paste by mixing 1 part of iron acetate liquor (prepared as recipe on left) with 8 parts of gum tragacanth or Nafka for screen printing or British gum or Nafka for block printing.

(d) Print, dry, hang for 48 hours or steam for 1 hour.

(e) Rinse under the cold tap, wash in hot soapy water, rinse in cold water, dry and iron on the reverse.

MANGANESE

Gives a dark sepia brown on cottons and linen.

Requirements

A plastic dyebath, smooth stirring rods, spoons, etc. Sodium or potassium dichromate (**poison**), manganese chloride, sodium acetate.

Method

(a) Mix, when required for use,
2 level teaspoons of sodium or potassium dichromate (poison) with 12 level teaspoons of prepared Nafka gum thickening. To dissolve completely, boil up and stir constantly.
Allow to cool and then add $2\frac{1}{2}$ level teaspoons of manganese chloride and $\frac{1}{2}$ level teaspoon of sodium acetate dissolved in 2 level teaspoons of water.
(b) Print, dry, and either air, hang or steam for 1 hour.
(c) Rinse in cold water, wash in hot soapy water, rinse in cold water, dry and iron on the reverse.

NOTE: This can be adjusted to paint on starch 'resist' or wax batik or discharged with citric acid or lemon juice.

NATURAL DYES —VEGETABLE
Indigo

To give blues and greys on cottons, silk and wool.

DYEING—HYDROSULPHITE VAT METHOD
Requirements

For small amounts of fabric, a large (3 gallon or more) plastic bucket placed inside a larger metal container with rubber or plastic foam interlining to insulate and retain the heat in the dyebath. Use deep rather than shallow containers.

For large amounts, a 10 gallon plastic dustbin within a larger metal dustbin with insulation between.

Indigo grains 60%; caustic soda flake; sodium hydrosulphite (sodium dithionide); common or sea salt, detergent (Stergene, Teepol, Lissapol ND, Washing Agent 5892 (GB), Synthrapol or Duponal (USA)), warm and cold water. Smooth stirring rods, spoons, rag, rubber gloves etc. Heating ring, drying facilities.

Method—Small amounts—Stock solution

(a) To 1 pint of cold water, *slowly* stir in 6 level teaspoons of caustic soda flake; this becomes very hot.
(b) To 1 pint of warm water, carefully stir in 6 level tablespoons of indigo grains; avoid undue disturbance of the surface.
(c) Add (a) to (b) very gently; a scum will form.
(d) Gradually add 3 level teaspoons of sodium hydrosulphite and gently stir as before.
(e) Leave for about 5 minutes.

THE DYEBATH

Add $\frac{1}{2}$ level teaspoon of sodium hydrosulphite to 2 gallons of warm soft water.

THE VAT

(a) Gently pour $\frac{1}{2}$ of the stock solution into another container, cover and place on one side for future use.
(b) Gently add the remaining $\frac{1}{2}$ of the stock solution to the dyebath by half-submerging the stock pot and tipping until the liquid in the dyebath and stockpot are level. The stock can then float out without forming bubbles.
This is essential since the dyeing property of the vat depends upon the exclusion of oxygen.

(c) Slowly raise the temperature of the vat to 50°C. *It is important not to exceed 60°C or the whole vat may be rendered useless.*

After 10–15 minutes, the vat liquor will turn a clear yellow. A shiny, purple metallic surface to the liquor means a good vat. Turn off heat. For Batik, allow the vat to cool down sufficiently for the wax not to be affected.

GENERAL NOTES

1. If the vat turns thick and milky or shows white spots, add a drop of caustic solution, until the vat becomes clear yellow again.

2. If the vat shows blue spots in a yellow liquor, add a few drops of hydrosulphite solution until the vat becomes clear yellow again.

(d) Prepare the fabric by squeezing in a solution of detergent and cold water. Prepare an open, weighted cradle of string or thread to hold the fabric below the vat surface during dyeing.

(e) Put the evenly damp fabric into the vat until it is totally immersed. Leave for 15 minutes for piece dyeing.

For tie-dyeing, 2 minutes or more will suffice.

GENERAL NOTES

1. Take great care to avoid as far as possible introducing bubbles of air trapped within the folds of the fabric or skeins of wool.

2. Do all the dippings slowly and without undue movement of the vat liquor.

3. Do not disturb the sediment at the bottom of the vat.

(f) *Carefully* remove the fabric from the vat. It should appear a brilliant yellow, changing rapidly to green and finally into permanent blue. This can take up to $\frac{1}{2}$ hour depending on local conditions. The fabric is best spread out or hung (in the open width for piece dyeing) to preserve an even dyeing.

(g) When the fabric is an even blue all over, it should be re-immersed in the vat (again avoiding bubbles of air or undue agitation of vat liquor). Follow the procedure for the first dip and oxidize in the air as before.

(h) In this way a series of dips will gradually deepen the shade and quality of the blue. The more dips, and the longer the length of time taken in each dip, the faster and richer the final colour.

(i) After the required depth of shade is reached, rinse the fabric well in running cold water. The final treatment is a wash in hot, soapy water. Rinse, dry and iron as required.

Method—Large amounts—Stock solution

(a) Place 2 cups of cold water in a bowl and *slowly* stir in 1 cup of caustic soda flake; this becomes very hot.

(b) To 5 pints of warm water in another container, add *gradually* 2 cups of indigo grains 60%; avoid undue disturbance of the surface.

(c) Add (a) to (b) very gently as before, a scum will form.

(d) Gradually add $1\frac{1}{2}$ cups of sodium hydrosulphite and gently stir as before.

(e) Leave for about 10 minutes.

THE DYEBATH

Add 1 cup of common salt (preferably sea salt) and $\frac{1}{4}$ cup of sodium hydrosulphite to 10 gallons of warm, soft water.

Prepare the vat and dye as for small amounts.

GENERAL NOTES

1. Continual dyeing gradually exhausts the vat, particularly if a great deal of oxygen is taken down into the vat with the fabric, or the vat is over-agitated. The vat liquor will change from a clear yellowish green to a grey liquid containing many specks of solidified indigo. Any fabric still in the vat at this stage should be removed.

The vat may be revived by adding $\frac{1}{3}$ of the remaining $\frac{1}{2}$ of the stock solution, well before the vat becomes dead and between the stages (f) and (g). After adding the stock solution raise the temperature of the vat to around 50°C for about 1 hour, stirring *very* gently. Allow to cool and re-immerse the fabric as before.

After a further use of the vat, another $\frac{1}{3}$ of the stock solution may be added as above, and so on.

After about 3 revivals the vat will be completely reduced by the hydrosulphite and then it becomes exhausted and tends to withdraw the indigo from the fabric being dyed.

2 level teaspoons of common salt dissolved in a little boiling water and added to the liquor will finally exhaust the vat at the end of dyeing.

2. For most dyeing, 6 dips is reasonable. Some dyers go up to 20 or more. Primitive peoples often used 40 dips as a normal dyeing procedure.

Indigo blue properly built up has a strange, metallic sheen unobtainable by other means.

3. A cooler dyebath, as used for batik dyeing, will retard the dyeing but give a more even dye. A hot dyebath (but *not* above 60°C) is quicker, but tends to give patchier results. This may not matter with tie dyes.

4. Caustic soda harshens and weakens wool and reduces the lustre of silk if used in excess.

Employ the minimum necessary for satisfactory dyeing. Caustic has little effect on cotton.

5. Acids weaken cottons but have little effect on silk and wool when used normally.

6. In tie-dyeing, untying and further tying may be carried out after oxidization and before further dippings.

7. $1\frac{1}{2}$ level teaspoons of ammonia added to the vat liquor for small amounts of fabric will give a redder blue.

8. A glass rod dipped into the vat quickly shows the colour.

9. Natural indigo is almost unobtainable nowadays. It has been replaced by synthetic indigo in a variety of forms, e.g. indigo grains, powdered or ground indigo or indigo paste.

10. Another method employs indigo extract. This is not a fast form of dyeing and is not recommended.

11. It is usually advisable to dye with indigo *before* other dyes such as rust (to produce browns) or walnut (to give blacks).

12. Vats should be kept covered when not in use to retard oxidization.

Walnut
A useful natural dye on wool and prepared cotton for converting indigo to black or as a brown substantive dye in its own right needing no mordant.

Requirements
Large dyebath, smooth stirring rods, spoons, rag, rubber gloves, heating ring, drying facilities, soap, cold water and, if used with a mordant, alum or cream of tartar.

Method without Mordant
(a) Collect walnuts when ripe, put shells *and* husks in a double muslin bag into a wood or plastic container and cover with soft water. The longer they steep the deeper the brown obtained.
(b) Further colour will be extracted by boiling for a long time. Strain the liquor.
(c) Prepare the fabric by squeezing in a solution of detergent and cold water.
(d) Immerse the evenly damp fabric and simmer in the dye liquor (add extra water to cover fabric) until as much of the dye has been absorbed as required (1–2 hours). Move the fabric gently during dyeing. Remove, rinse, wash in a hot soapy solution, rinse and dry.

Method with Mordant
This dye can also be mordanted with alum to produce a brighter brown, as follows: —
(a) Allow $\frac{3}{4}$ oz. of alum plus $1\frac{1}{2}$ oz. of cream of tartar per 1 lb. weight of dry fabric. Bring to the boil in a little water and stir until thoroughly dissolved.
(b) Stir this mixture into sufficient water to cover the fabric well (up to 3 gallons).
(c) Immerse the prepared and evenly damp fabric (which can be undyed or already dyed). Raise to boiling (simmer only for silk) in 1–$1\frac{1}{2}$ hours and simmer for $\frac{1}{2}$ hour.
(d) Rinse in 3 very hot waters, squeeze out and dye in a day or so if the fabric has not already been dyed.

GENERAL NOTES
1. Walnut is not suitable for fine soft wool, it tends to make it harsh.
2. Dye the fabric with indigo first and walnut second to obtain a black.

Cutch (Kutch or Catecu)
To give yellows and browns. Is particularly good for cottons, and is also used for wool. It requires a mordant and gives different shades on different mordants.

Requirements
Large dyebath, smooth stirring rods, spoons, rag, rubber gloves, heating ring, drying facilities, soap, cold water.
If used with alum as a mordant—alum and cream of tartar. With tin-stannous chloride and cream of tartar. With iron-ferrous sulphate and a special dyebath kept for iron mordant. With chrome-bichromate of potash.

Method
(a) Cutch comes as dark brown lumps. If these become damp they go sticky and are difficult to break up.
(b) Boil up to dissolve and pour the solution (but not dregs) into the dyebath adding sufficient water to well cover the evenly damp fabric which should be immersed (prepared if undyed) in the dyebath and either steeped all night or brought to the boil and simmered for about 1 hour.
(c) Then mordant. These give a variety of effects.
(1) Alum gives a yellow brown (see walnut for alum mordanting recipe).
(2) Tin and cream of tartar gives brown yellow.

Recipe for (2)
Some cream of tartar (say 2 oz.) dissolved in water in the dyebath and $\frac{1}{2}$ oz. of stannous chloride added and stirred in. Immerse the evenly damp fabric and slowly raise to the boil and simmer for 1 hour. Remove, rinse. Particularly suitable for wool (but do not boil).

(3) Iron gives a variety of greys. Some may be developed by dyeing with weak cutch/strong mordant; weak cutch/weak mordant; strong mordant/strong cutch; weak cutch/weak mordant/weak cutch will all give varying colours. The mordanting can be done by cold steeping or hot mordanting which again varies the final colour.

Recipe for (3)
$\frac{1}{4}$ to 2 ozs. of ferrous sulphate, ground to a fine powder and dissolved in cold water then filtered off to leave the sediment and the filtered solution put in a special dyebath kept for iron mordanting. The dye liquor in which the fabric has been dyed is poured into this iron dyebath, stirring all the time. The evenly damp fabric is immersed and gently moved and the simmering is continued for 15 or more minutes. The fabric is then removed, soaped, washed, rinsed and dried.

(4) Chrome gives a plain chocolate brown which makes a good black if dyed on an indigo dyeing. It is best used after the dyeing in cutch or, if mordanted, before and after dyeing.

Recipe for (4)
Dissolve $\frac{1}{4}$ to $\frac{1}{2}$ oz. of bichromate of potash in a little hot water (boil if necessary) and add to required amount of hot water in a dyebath. Immerse hot/wet dyed fabric, place a lid on the dyebath and slowly bring to the boil. Simmer for 1 hour or longer, remove and rinse at once in hot water.

Logwood & Young's Fast Black (a preparation of logwood and mordant).
Suitable for wool, cotton, linen and silk. Gives blacks, greys, blue-greys and purples.

Dyeing Method—Wool
For blacks and greys on wool
(a) 1 lb. of wool is mordanted (after an initial preparation of squeezing in a solution of detergent and cold water) with $\frac{1}{2}$ oz. of bichromate of potash (see alum recipe on page 132). Rinse thoroughly after mordanting in bichromate of potash.
(b) 8 ozs. of logwood is dissolved in a bath of warm water. The evenly damp and mordanted wool is immersed, brought up to, but not beyond the boil and dyed for at least 1 hour. Remove and wash thoroughly.

GENERAL NOTES
1. A few drops of sulphuric acid added *to* the mordant will make the black more intense.
2. Cutch or walnut added to the mordant will give a dark brown/black.
3. $\frac{1}{2}$ oz. of fustic chips added to the mordant will give a flat neutral black. Mordant for $1\frac{1}{2}$ hours. Wash after mordanting.
4. For a grey, enter the evenly damp wool into a mordant bath of $\frac{1}{2}$ oz. of bichromate of potash and 1 oz. cream of tartar for about 15 minutes, then remove it. Add 4 ozs. of logwood (already boiled for $\frac{1}{2}$ hour). Re-enter the wool and simmer for 30 minutes. Remove and wash.
5. For a blue-grey—mordant with alum and cream of tartar. 3 ozs. of logwood and $\frac{1}{2}$ oz. of bichromate of potash dissolved in hard water (add chalk to soft water) to make the dyebath. The evenly damp wool is immersed and kept almost at boiling point for nearly 1 hour, then removed and washed.
6. Logwood chips should always be steeped in the dyebath in a fine muslin bag to prevent pieces of the wood remaining in the bath. $\frac{1}{2}$ lb. of chips equals 1 oz. of logwood extract.

Dyeing Method—Cotton

For grey and purple on cotton already prepared by boiling in detergent and water:

(a) Steep 1 lb. dry weight cotton yarn or fabric in a bath of a strong solution of 1 oz. tannic acid to enough water to cover the fabric. Bring to boiling point and simmer for $\frac{1}{2}$ hour. Remove from the heat and allow the fabric to cool in the liquor in the bath for several hours. Remove and wash. This is called 'galling the fabric'.

(b) For grey, dye with 4 ozs. logwood at boiling point for 1 hour. Mordant in another dyebath with bichromate of potash and cream of tartar. Remove and wash.

(c) For purple, mordant with iron (see page 133). Then mordant in a different bath with tin (see page 133).

Then dye with 3 ozs. of logwood at boiling point for 1 hour.

Many other logwood recipes will be found in Ethel Mairet's *A Book on Vegetable Dyes*.

Screening Method

Screen, block or pad printing with Young's Fast Black for cotton and linen.

(a) 3 parts of Fast Black stirred into 12 parts of starch thickening (Nafka gum or gum tragacanth) to which a few drops of acetic acid (40%) have been added.

(b) Print the fabric, dry, steam for 1 hour.

(c) Rinse in cold water, wash in hot, soapy water, rinse, dry, and iron on the reverse.

PIGMENT COLOURS

Are suitable for most fabrics except wool and pile cloths. They should be printed as thinly as possible onto the fabric to avoid stiffness after fixation. This will be particularly noticeable on fine fabrics such as silk or lawn.

Printex (GB) (Formerly known as Tinolite (GB))

1 part (for pale shade)–3 parts (for deep shades) of Printex pigment colour added to 100 parts of Printex Binder CM 18%. Stir well,

or approximately 1 level teaspoon (pale) –3 level teaspoons of (deep) pigment– $\frac{3}{4}$ of a lb. jam jar of binder. Stir well, if necessary, sieve. Adjust with more binder for screening, less for block printing.

Polyprint (GB) or Aquaprint (USA)

$\frac{1}{20}$ part (pale)–1 part of (deep) Polyprint pigment added to 9 parts of (deep) Polyprint binder. Stir well.

GENERAL NOTES

1. For fluorescent colours use 1 part of fluorescent pigment–10 parts binder. Stir well.

2. For metallic prints use 1 part of silver powder–9 parts of Metallic binder GS or 2 parts of gold powder–8 parts of Metallic binder GS. Stir well. (Use a screen covering, gauge 8 or larger, to prevent screen blocking.)

3. White WP may be printed without binder for very dense white effects.

Helizarin (GB) or Alizarin (USA)

1. *For pad printing*

1 level teaspoon of Condensol A dissolved in 1 level teaspoon of cold water in a 1 lb. jam jar, $\frac{3}{4}$ of a 1 lb. jam jar of binder D added to the above. 1 level teaspoon (pale)–4 level teaspoons (deep) of Helizarin colour added to the jam jar. Stir thoroughly.

2. *For Screen printing adapt recipe as follows:*—

1 level teaspoon of Condensol A dissolved in 1 level teaspoon of cold water in a 1 lb. jam jar, 1 level teaspoon (pale)–4 level teaspoons (deep) of Helizarin colour added to the above. To this is added a

mixture of 24 level teaspoons of reduction binder and 12 level teaspoons of binder D. All are then mixed very thoroughly.

3. Special recipes are available from the suppliers for white screen prints on dark shades, metallic prints, luminous colours, nylon and terylene printing.

METHOD FOR PRINTING AND FIXATION OF ALL THE ABOVE PIGMENT COLOURS.

(a) Stir well and print. All colours in each range can be intermixed.

(b) Do not leave screens or blocks or pads with mixed colour on them without using, for longer than 10 minutes, the colour may dry and block the screen. Although soluble in water when liquid, pigment colours gradually harden in the air and can be exceedingly difficult to remove. If you have to leave your printing for more than this time, wash out screens etc., with cold water.

(c) Screen blocking can partly be avoided when using a Printex paste mixture by adding 1 or 2 level teaspoons of glycerine to the paste mixture. Cool printing conditions will assist all pigment colours to work easily.

(d) Flow, in the case of Printex, Polyprint or Aquaprint can be adjusted by the addition of a little Manutex RS 5% thickening to the print paste mixture.

(e) After printing allow to dry *thoroughly,* preferably overnight, and fix by:

either (1) ironing for 4/5 minutes over every part of the reverse of the print at the correct temperature for the fabric used,

or (2) Baking for 4/5 minutes at 130°C (250°F) in an electric oven (longer for big items folded several times),

or (3) In the case of Polyprint and Aquaprint, steam for 1 hour in a steamer.

(f) After fixation there is no need to wash the printed fabric but all apparatus should be washed up in cold water as soon as possible with a weak detergent solution, then rinsed and wiped dry.

GENERAL NOTES

1. As the pigments contain small amounts of toxic materials only ready mixed colours should be given to young children.

2. Avoid smoking or naked lights whilst handling these colours as the solvent used is inflammable at 300°C. Ensure good ventilation and cool working conditions.

3. Once mixed the pastes retain their full strength up to 2 weeks if kept in the cool in screw-topped containers.

Prang Aqua Pigments (USA)

Are suitable for all fabrics except pile and velvet.

(a) Just add any necessary cold water to the colour paste (from the jar) required by the particular technique (pad, block, potato, screen, stencil, brush, etc.) to be used.

(b) Colours can all be intermixed or toner used to reduce the strength of a colour.

(c) Fix the colour by letting the fabric dry, then covering with a cloth and ironing for 3 minutes at 175°C (350°F) for cotton or linen, 5 minutes at 121°C (250°F) for silk, wool, rayon. Each part of the fabric must receive its full time or ironing. It is better to overheat or iron longer than to underheat although avoid scorching or damaging the cloth. Repeat ironing on the reverse side.

(d) Wash out everything used with cold water.

(e) The unused colours can be returned to their jars.

Tri-chem (GB)

Use direct from ball point 'marker'-type holder. Allow to dry, iron at fabric heat. Useful for drawing thin lines.

Fabricol (GB)

These dyes are in a thin paste form and colours are intermixable. No preparation is required; the dyes are ready for application. Brushes, screens, blocks etc., are washed in water after use. The 'Fabricol' base is used to dilute the colour but retain the viscosity. The fixer is a clear viscous liquid (replace the screw-cap when not in use). Fabricol dyes are suitable for all purpose cottons, linens, calicos and silks. Viscose rayon is suitable but acetate rayon, nylon, terylene, and materials with synthetic finishes (i.e. drip-dry) are not suitable unless thoroughly scoured.

The dyes can be applied by any method. Providing the dye covers the fabric, the thickness of application is not important; any surplus dye will wash out.

When the design has been completed, the fabric must be left until the dyes are completely dry. Artificial drying can be effected if required.

Always work on a clean surface.

The fixer is applied liberally over the whole of the surface of the fabric to which the dye has been applied. A two or three-inch varnish or paint brush is suitable.

When the fixer has been applied, fold the fabric face-to-face, corner-to-corner, then continue to fold until of a convenient size to fit into a plastic bag. The purpose of the plastic bag is to exclude the air from the fabric and to prevent the fixer from drying. Leave the fabric with fixer in the plastic bag for a minimum of two hours. The fabric can be left in the bag for any subsequent length of time (i.e. over a week-end) always providing that the bag is properly airtight and that the fixer does not dry.

To wash away the fixer and the surplus dye, take the fabric from the bag, fully unfold and rinse in a sink of warm soapy water. Work the fabric in the water with your hands until the water is well coloured (i.e. surplus dye coming away from material). Replace with clean warm or cold water and proceed as with the first rinse; 2 or 3 changes of water may be required. Make sure that the fixer and all surplus dye are washed out. Squeeze fabric as dry as possible. Hang, or preferably lay flat to dry.

When dry, the fabric can be treated as any other fabric. It can be ironed, machine-washed, spin-dried, etc.

Fabricol dyes, base and fixer are non-toxic. They have good colour permanence and will not produce any stiffening in the fabric.

REACTIVE DYES

Are suitable for cellulose fibres and, particularly, mercerised cotton, and linen and viscose rayon. Certain of the dyes will dye wool, silk, nylon and some acrylic fibres and newer ranges are constantly being discovered.

It is probable that this class of dyestuffs will supersede most other dyes at present in use. They are very simple to apply and give an outstanding range of bright colours, exceedingly fast to light and washing. This is achieved because the dyes are soluble in water and the dye molecules make a direct chemical link with the fibre. It is generally necessary for a weak alkali to be present in the dyebath.

The range is divided into 2 groups:
Group 1 (Procion M) is much more reactive than the other group and does not require steaming to fix the dye. This has great advantages in batik work. In tie and dye the ties need to be tight as the dyes penetrate very readily.

Group 2 brand names include Procions (Procion H, Procion Supra, Procinyl, all ICI); Cibacrons (CIBA); Reactones

(Geigy); Remazols (Hoechst AG) and Drimarenes (Sandoz).

One essential when Reactives are used is the final washing off process after fixation. This must be very thorough to remove all surplus loose dye still resting in the fibres.

Cibacrons

Are suitable for cottons, linen, viscose rayon, natural silk and chlorinated wool.

PIECE & TIE DYEING

Method

Add the required amount of dye, which has been dissolved in a little water, to the bath. (The suitable amount of water is about 30 times the weight of the dry cloth to be dyed; the water should always cover the cloth in the dye bath.) Heat to 40°C, add 20 level teaspoonsful of common salt dissolved in 1 quart of water and 1 level teaspoonful of caustic soda flake dissolved in 1 quart of water.

Immerse the evenly damp fabric, raise the temperature over 15 minutes to 75°C and dye for 30 minutes. Rinse, then wash in detergent until clear. After dyeing thoroughly clean the dyebath.

NOTE

(1) A variation, particularly for deep tones, is not to add the caustic soda *before* the fabric but at the point when the dyebath has reached 75°C and then to dye for 45 minutes.

(2) Bath dyeing is known technically as the 'Exhaust Method' and those Cibacron dyes best suited to this form have a suffix -E or -A (others with -P mean pad form of dyeing, -D means printing).

SCREEN PRINTING for cotton and viscose rayon.

Steaming Method

(a) 1 (pale)–3 (deep) level teaspoons of dye pasted with

(b) 22 level teaspoons of hot water, if necessary boil up.

(c) 9 level teaspoons of urea are stirred in.

This mixture is then stirred into:

(d) 12 level teaspoons of Manutex RS 5% thickening (note 3). When ready to print stir in,

(e) 1½ level teaspoons of sodium bicarbonate (2½ for Turquoise Blue & Black) and 1 level teaspoon of Resist Salt C (Albatex BD) which have all been pasted together in a little cold water.

(f) Print, dry and steam for 10–15 minutes.

(g) Rinse thoroughly, first in cold water, then hot water (60°C) followed by 5 minutes at the boil in a solution of ½ level teaspoon of washing Agent 6892–1 quart of water.

Rinse, dry and iron on the reverse.

GENERAL NOTES

1. With steaming method, Cibacron Black BG-A gives a better black.

2. Baking can also be used to fix Cibacron dyes. The recipe requires double the amount of urea. Best results are obtained on cotton and should be carried out for 4 minutes at 150°C.

3. Adjust the amount of Manutex and/or water to obtain suitable screen printing consistency.

4. Any tendency to acidity in the thickener may be neutralized with 2 or 3 drops of ammonia.

5. Black with clean, sharp edges can be mixed from 6 parts Cibacron 2RA and 2 parts Cibacron Golden Yellow F2RA.

SCREEN PRINTING for natural silk and chlorinated wool.

Steaming Method.

(a) This recipe is as for cotton but the amount of urea is decreased to 6 level teaspoons, the thickener increased to 14 level teaspoons and the sodium bicarbonate must not exceed $1\frac{1}{2}$ level teaspoons for any dye.

(b) Silk will require 15 minutes steaming followed by a thorough rinse first in cold water and then in hot water. The print is then treated for 10 minutes in $\frac{1}{2}$ level teaspoon of ammonia–1 pint water at 60°C, rinsed and neutralized in $\frac{1}{4}$ level teaspoonful of formic acid 85%–1 pint of cold water, then dried and ironed on the reverse.

N.B. Use Cibacron Black BG-A on silk.

SCREEN PRINTING for cotton, viscose rayon, natural silk and chlorinated wool
Catalyst Method
(a) 1 (pale)–3 (deep, 5 for black, note 2) level teaspoons of dye pasted with
(b) 18 level teaspoons of hot water, if necessary boil up.
(c) 12 level teaspoons of urea are stirred in. The mixture is then stirred into:
(d) 10–30 level teaspoons of Manutex RS 5% thickening (note 3). When ready to print, stir in:—
(e) 2 level teaspoons ($1\frac{1}{2}$ when on silk or wool) sodium bicarbonate and 2 level teaspoons of Catalyst CC1 and 1 level teaspoon of Resist Salt C (Albatex BD) which have been pasted together in a little cold water.
(f) Print, dry and iron for 30 seconds on the appropriate fabric setting.
(g) After fixing, rinse well in cold water, then hot water, followed by 5 minutes at the boil in $\frac{1}{2}$ level teaspoon of washing agent 6892–1 quart of water. Rinse, dry and iron on the reverse.

GENERAL NOTES
1. If the fabric printed by the Catalyst method is steamed and *not* ironed, the duration of steaming should not exceed 2 minutes.

2. With the Catalyst method Cibacron Black 2P-D gives a better black.
3. Adjust the amount of Manutex and/or water to obtain the suitable screen printing consistency.
4. Suitable for Batik (see next section but one).

BLOCK AND PAD PRINTING, DIRECT PAINTING.
Any of the screen recipes may be used for these forms as long as the amount of Manutex is reduced by $\frac{1}{2}$ for Block and Pad or by $\frac{3}{4}$ or Direct Painting or as required for the particular technique used. (See General notes on Reactive Dyes, particularly 1 and 2).

BATIK
Catalyst Method
The Catalyst method is very appropriate for this technique. The mixing of recipes for particular fibres may be followed up to Section (f). The mixed dyestuff is painted on the fabric on top of the solid or cracked wax and allowed to dry. The fabric is then ironed for 30 seconds between several layers of newspapers with the appropriate fabric setting. This not only fixes the dye but also irons out the wax. Change the paper frequently. The fabric is rinsed etc., as in the original recipe.

GENERAL NOTES
1. Where it is desired to steam to fix the dye, this may still be done using the steaming methods already given as long as the wax is ironed off between paper which is changed frequently. The fabric is then fixed and rinsed etc., as in the original recipe.
2. Similarly, if baking in an electric oven is used to fix the dye, follow the appropriate steaming recipe but double the amount

of urea used. The wax should be ironed off before baking for 4 minutes at 150°C. Best results are obtained on cotton.

Procions — Procion M (should not be intermixed with Procion H dyes)

Are suitable for mercerised cotton and viscose rayon and may also be used for linen, cottons, natural silk and chlorinated wool to give slightly paler shades.

PIECE DYEING
Long Dyeing Method
For dry fabric weighing up to $\frac{1}{4}$ lb.
(a) $\frac{1}{8}$ level teaspoon Procion M dye for pale shades
$\frac{1}{4}$ level teaspoon Procion M dye for medium shades
$\frac{1}{2}$ level teaspoon Procion M dye for deep shades.
(b) Paste the dye with a little cold water. Add sufficient warm water up to 1 pint (keeping it below 70°C) until a clear solution is obtained.
(c) Add the dissolved dye as (b) to 5 pints of cold water.
(d) Immerse the washed and rinsed fabric whilst still wet in (c) and dye for 10–15 minutes on a low heat, keep turning the fabric. Add 4 level tablespoons of common salt to the dyebath gradually over the next 15 minutes.
Add $3\frac{1}{2}$ level teaspoons of washing soda crystals (or 2 level teaspoons of anhydrous sodium carbonate) and keep the fabric turning well for a total of 1 hour at 40°C (Procion Navy Blue M-3R at 60°C).
(e) After dyeing, rinse well in cold water then wash for 15 minutes in Lissapol ND ($\frac{1}{2}$ level teaspoon–1 quart of water). Cottons may be boiled off but boiling will harshen other fabrics. Rinse again and dry.
Thorough washing is essential to remove surplus dye and prevent later marking-off.

(f) The dye liquor *cannot be used again.* The dyebath and any mixing sticks, bowls etc., should be washed out as soon as possible in cold water.

BATIK AND PIECE DYEING
Short Dyeing Method
For dry fabric weighing up to $\frac{1}{4}$ lb.
(a) $\frac{1}{2}$ level teaspoon Procion M dye for pale shades
$1\frac{1}{4}$ level teaspoons Procion M dye for medium shades
2 level teaspoons Procion M dye for deep shades.
(b) Paste the dye with a little cold water. Add sufficient warm water up to $\frac{1}{2}$ pint (keeping it below 70°C) until a clear solution is obtained.
(c) Dissolve $1\frac{1}{2}$ level teaspoons of common salt or urea in 1 pint of cold water.
(d) Mix (b) and (c) together in a large shallow bowl.
(e) Immerse the fabric in a large bowl for 5 minutes and turn well. Only add more water if it is required to cover the fabric.
(f) Dissolve 3 level teaspoons of washing soda (or $1\frac{1}{2}$ level teaspoons of anhydrous sodium carbonate) in about $\frac{1}{8}$ pint of warm water and add to a large bowl containing the fabric.
Leave for a further 15 minutes, turning as before.
(g) Wearing rubber gloves gently squeeze out the surplus dye
either (i) Lay the wet but unrinsed fabric on newspaper on the floor overnight. (The steam from a kettle boiled for a few moments near to the fabric will shorten the fixation time.)
or (ii) The wet but unrinsed fabric may be placed in a plastic bag or rolled in plastic for 2–3 hours.
or (iii) The wet but unrinsed fabric may be placed in a cupboard or a very large box and the steam from a boiling kettle

directed into the cupboard for a few minutes. After about 1 hour the fabric will be fixed.

(h) Rinse well. Wash thoroughly (or boil for cottons) for 5 minutes in Lissapol ND, Stergene, Teepol (GB), Synthrapol or Duponal (USA) ($\frac{1}{2}$ level teaspoon–1 quart of water). Rinse and iron.

(i) Dye mixed with salt and soda remains potent for $1-1\frac{1}{2}$ hours only. Do not attempt to use again or store the dye after that time.

(j) Clear up at once with cold water.

(k) Avoid splashing the dye on clothes, hands, floor etc. It stains and is very difficult to remove. Cover tables and floor with newspaper.

Brentamine Fast Black K Salt

Will react with most Procion dyes to produce rich, dark brown shades. After waxing and dyeing in batik work and *before* fixation the Brentamine should be painted onto the fabric or the fabric dipped into a solution of Brentamine prepared as one or other of the following recipes. It can of course be resisted by wax or painted on with a brush if thickened with prepared Manutex RS 5% thickening.

RECIPE A

1 level teaspoon of Brentamine Fast Black K Salt dissolved in $\frac{1}{3}$ pint of water.

RECIPE B

1 or 2 level teaspoons of Brentamine Fast Black K Salt dissolved in $2\frac{1}{2}$ level teaspoons of acetic acid with $6\frac{1}{2}$ level teaspoons of water and $1\frac{1}{2}$ level teaspoons of Manutex thickening.

Black Procion M Dye is not marketed as such but may be mixed from other Procion M dyes as follows:

$3\frac{1}{4}$ level teaspoons Navy Blue M-3RS

1 level teaspoon Yellow M4-RS

$\frac{3}{4}$ level teaspoon Brilliant Red M-5BS

This can be well mixed when dry and then prepared as the particular recipe given above.

Variations in the amount of yellow used in this recipe will produce interesting and unusual dark browns and greys.

SCREEN, BLOCK & PAD PRINTING
(cottons, linen, rayon)

As particular patterns will use more or less of a dye paste, it is not possible to give the yardage of fabric. The following recipe will make about 1 pint of dye paste ready for printing.

(a) 1 level teaspoon Procion M dye for pale shades

3 level teaspoons Procion M dye for medium shades

5 level teaspoons Procion M dye for deep shades.

(b) Paste the dye with a little cold water.

(c) 10 level teaspoons of urea dissolved in $\frac{1}{2}$ pint of water which may be heated up to but not above 70°C.

(d) Dissolve (b) in (c).

(e) Slowly stir this mixture into 1 oz. of Manutex RS 5% thickening.

THE ABOVE WILL KEEP AS IT IS FOR SEVERAL DAYS

(f) Just before printing stir in the alkali which is

either $1\frac{1}{2}$ level teaspoons of sodium bicarbonate pasted in a little cold water *if fixation method is (h) 1, 2 or 3.*

or $\frac{1}{2}$ level teaspoon of anhydrous sodium carbonate and 1 level teaspoon of sodium bicarbonate pasted in a little cold water *if fixation method is (h) 4.*

AFTER ALKALI IS ADDED THE DYE PASTE WILL REMAIN AT FULL STRENGTH FOR $1-1\frac{1}{2}$ HOURS ONLY.

(g) Print, then dry to remove moisture.

(h) (1) Steam 5–10 minutes
or (2) Bake 5 minutes at 140°C in an ordinary electric oven
or (3) Iron 5 minutes at 140°C on the reverse with a steam iron
or (4) Air hang 24–48 hours in a warm humid atmosphere (i.e. boil a kettle in the room for some moments).

After fixing, rinse thoroughly for 5 minutes (in as open a width as possible) in running water to remove all the loose colour. Boil or wash for 5 minutes in clean water, repeat the boiling with fresh water if required. IF NECESSARY boil or wash for 5 minutes in Lissapol ND, Stergene, Teepol (GB), Synthrapol or Duponal (USA) ($\frac{1}{2}$ level teaspoon in 1 quart of water). When clean, rinse and dry. Thorough washing is essential to complete the printing process. Never leave the printed fabric soaking or half washed, but continue until the whites are clear.

(i) An alternative method is to thoroughly scour the fabric, soak it for 1 minute in a cold solution of 4 teaspoons of common soda crystals to 1 pint of water. Squeeze out fabric, dry and iron down ready for printing. The Procion M print paste should then be applied *without* the alkali in (f) above. After printing dry and fix as in (g) and (h).

(j) Clear up at once with cold water.

DIRECT PAINTING

The above recipes that include thickening may all be used but the amount of thickening should be halved or altered until the dye paste flows from the brush.

FOR SILK & CHLORINATED WOOL

(i) Manutex F thickening gives better definition to prints than Manutex RS on silks and wools.

(ii) Steaming time should be the full 10 minutes and the steam should be as dry as possible.

(iii) If steam is rather wet then decrease the amount of urea in recipe.

(iv) Steaming is advised rather than any other methods of fixing.

(v) Omit the sodium bicarbonate when printing on wool.

(vi) Do not increase the alkali at all when printing on silk.

Turquoise Blue is not a Procion M colour. Procion Brilliant Blue H-5GS may be used for screen printing but only for methods 1, 2 or 3, of fixing (*not* the air hanging method).

GENERAL NOTES ON REACTIVE DYES

1. Procion dyes are not suitable for starch vegetables in pad printing except as a form of discharge or resist printing. The starch content prevents the Procion developing in the fabric. However, this can be utilized in the design to produce textured prints.

2. The chemicals used in the dye recipes will dissolve the usual mordant used when flocking lino blocks. This mordant should be replaced with *either* Bedafin 2001 and the block heated in an oven after flocking for 5 minutes at 135°C (275°F) *or* an adhesive such as Clam, Bostik 2 (UK) or Sobo (USA).

3. Since these dyes are exceptionally fast and will stain almost anything it is advisable to use rubber gloves, plenty of newspaper on the tables, avoid scattering the dry powder and clear up as soon as possible with cold water.

4. The dyestuffs are in powder form and each dye may be mixed within the range in any proportion both for dyeing and printing but M and H ranges should NOT be intermixed.

5. Acid fumes near to Procion dyestuffs will adversely affect the development of those dyestuffs.

6. Procion M dye pastes should be prepared as required, but Procion H dye pastes can be stored in cool air-tight jars for 2–3 weeks if desired.

7. It is essential that all jars containing dyes and chemicals are kept closed and lids replaced immediately after use, otherwise water is absorbed from the air and this weakens the contents and leads to poor fixation on the fabric.

Procion H and **Procion Supra** dyes should not be intermixed with Procion M dyes.

Suitable for mercerized cotton and viscose rayon and may also be used for linen, cottons, natural silk and chlorinated wool to give slightly paler shades.

PIECE DYEING

For dry material weighing up to $\frac{1}{4}$ lb.

(a) $\frac{1}{8}$ level teaspoon of Procion H or Supra dye for pale shades
$\frac{1}{4}$ level teaspoon of Procion H or Supra dye for medium shades
$\frac{1}{2}$ level teaspoon of Procion H or Supra dye for deep shades.

It may be necessary to increase these quantities with some of the dyes and fabrics.

(b) Paste the dye with a little cold water. Add sufficient warm water up to 1 pint (keeping it below 70°C) until a clear solution is obtained.

(c) Add the dissolved dyestuff as (b) to 5 pints of cold water.

(d) Immerse the washed and rinsed fabric whilst still wet in (c) and dye for 10–15 minutes, keep turning the fabric.

Add 6 level teaspoons of common salt to the dyebath gradually over the next 15 minutes.

Add $17\frac{1}{2}$ level teaspoons of washing soda crystals (or 10 level teaspoons of anhydrous sodium carbonate) and keep the fabric turning well for a total of 1 hour at 85°C.

(e) After dyeing, rinse well in cold water then wash for 15 minutes in Lissapol ND ($\frac{1}{2}$ level teaspoon–1 quart of water). Cottons may be boiled off but boiling will harshen other fabrics. Rinse again and dry. Thorough washing is essential to remove the surplus dye and prevent later marking off.

(f) The dye liquor cannot be used again. The dyebath and any mixing sticks, bowls, etc., should be washed out as soon as possible in cold water.

SCREEN, BLOCK, PAD PRINTING & DIRECT PAINTING

Use the methods given for this form of printing in the appropriate section for Procion M dyes but Procion H or Supra dyes must be fixed by steaming, or ironing. They are not suitable for the air hanging method.

THICKENERS
Manutex RS (GB)

Suitable for all dyes and essential for Reactives.

Manutex RS 5% thickening is prepared as follows:

BLOCK PRINTING

$\frac{1}{4}$ level teaspoon of Calgon dissolved in 14 level teaspoons of warm water and $1\frac{1}{4}$ pints of cold water added.

4 level teaspoons of Manutex RS slowly sprinkled on this solution, stirring all the time and for a further 5–10 minutes to break down any lumps. After standing for 20–30 minutes (or preferably overnight) the thickening will become smooth and clear and ready for use. Straining is not normally necessary. Restir before use.

This thickener will keep for several weeks.

SCREEN PRINTING

As recipe above, but increase to 1 level tablespoon of Calgon and 4 level tablespoons of Manutex RS. Keep the method and amount of water the same as before.

DIRECT PAINTING

Either use less Manutex thickener with the dye

   or reduce Calgon to $\frac{1}{8}$ level teaspoon (see block printing recipe).

Manutex F (GB)

Similar to Manutex RS but gives a sharper definition to prints on silk and chlorinated wool. The recipe is as above but the quantity of Manutex F is 5 level teaspoons for Block printing and 5 level tablespoons for Screen printing.

GENERAL NOTES

1. The variations in the amount of Calgon for different purposes is to control the flow characteristics of the paste.

2. Manutex thickening and the print pastes incorporating them must not be boiled during preparation or printing.

Keltex S 5% (USA)

Suitable for all dyes and essential for Reactives.

SCREEN PRINTING

$1\frac{1}{4}$ level teaspoons of preservative (Dowicide A) and $\frac{3}{4}$ level teaspoon of ammonia 28%, added to $6\frac{1}{2}$ pints of cold water. 4 ozs. of improved Keltex S is sprinkled into the above solution under high speed agitation. After about $\frac{1}{2}$ hour of mixing, the paste is ready to use.

GENERAL NOTES

1. Thicken or thin with extra Keltex or water as required after the dyestuff has been added.

2. For Block printing the amount of Keltex S may be reduced to 1 oz. or the stock solution thinned with water.

3. Keltex thickening and the print pastes incorporating Keltex must not be boiled during preparation or printing.

Nafka Crystal Gum

Suitable for Acid and Direct dyes and the Discharge method, but not for Reactives like Procions and Cibacrons.

NORMAL METHOD

Sprinkle sufficient Nafka gum into cold water, stirring continuously until a thick mixture is obtained. Leave overnight. Then thin as required. It will keep 3–6 days depending on the humidity of the room.

QUICK METHOD

Boil $\frac{1}{2}$ a saucepan of water, remove from the heat and SLOWLY stir in enough gum to make a thick mixture. Return and STIR continuously over a GENTLE heat for a few minutes until all the gum has dissolved. Leave to cool, and if necessary, strain and remove any lumps. Soak the saucepan in cold water and clean up. Thin the gum with water as required. It will keep 3–6 days depending on the humidity of the room.

STAINS

If dye is accidentally dropped onto a fabric, remove at once any surplus carefully with a clean spoon or blunt knife. Keep the stain wet with a drop or two of cold water.

On a white fabric or one with a fast ground colour, the stain can be removed or reduced by Formosul or Dygon depending on the dischargeability of the dye. The Formosul or Dygon is mixed with cold water and applied to the stain, dried and then ironed with a steam iron between clean cloth or paper at a temperature safe for the fabric.

If the dye is non-dischargeable or the ground colour is not very fast and the stain will not be hidden by further printing it can be left until after processing and then covered with a white (or appropriately coloured) pigment dye such as Polyprint or Printex. This should be applied with a soft clean stencil brush and as thinly as possible to mask the stain.

DO NOT use household bleaches. Many of these contain chlorine which decomposes and/or discolours silk, wool and nylon. If concentrated, bleach will rot cotton, linen and rayons.

DO NOT use oxalic acid on silk or wool.

DO NOT use acetone or nail varnish remover on acetate rayon or tricel.

DO NOT use any grease solvent on plastics.

STEAMING EQUIPMENT AND PROCEDURE

One of the great advantages of fabric printing as a school or home craft is that excellent results can be obtained from simple materials and the processes may be simplified for the very young or the handicapped person.

It is possible to confine the processes to the wide variety of cold dyeing and printing techniques used in Batik and Pad printing with Dylon cold dyes and the Procion M range. Other dyes may be used with the hot dye bath methods for Piece dyeing and Tie and Dye.

Pigment dyes such as Polyprint and Printex or the Cibacron Catalyst method only require the use of a hot iron to fix them. These give a very wide and flexible range of dyestuffs and could cover all the techniques so far given in this book. However the serious student and craftsman will undoubtedly wish to use those dyes which do require a steaming process to complete the reaction of the dye and chemicals within the fibre.

Before steaming, the dye is still in the main lying trapped in a dried coating of thickener, on top of the fibre. During steaming, each printed area absorbs moisture from the steam and, in effect, becomes a very concentrated dyebath. It is then that the dye and chemicals penetrate and dye the fibre. The thickening helps to prevent the dye from spreading outside the printed shape. The appropriate steaming time can be exceeded if this cannot be avoided or it may be done in 2 parts provided that the fabric is kept dry between steamings.

Keeping dry is an important element in the fixation of dyes by steam. If the printed dye is still damp when wrapped for steaming, not only may it 'mark-off' on itself but as further moisture is absorbed, it may be too much for the dye and cause 'bleeding' by the dye into the surrounding background.

All the steaming cloths, pads, newspaper and the printed fabric itself should be as dry as possible before steaming. After steaming, the cloths and pads should be dried in open width and not left lying around in heaps. If put out whilst still hot from the steamer they will dry very quickly.

The apparatus can be very simple or elaborate and expensive.

The basic requirements are:

1. A container to hold sufficient water to boil for about 1 hour without replenishing.

2. A container perforated in the bottom to allow a reasonable flow of steam to pass up and around the wrapped parcel of printed goods inside the container, and out through a hole or holes in the lid. This receptacle should be placed over the water container as with a domestic vegetable or pudding steamer.

Many home-made containers do not give full 'fixation' because they do not supply sufficient steam.

More advanced types have the water container large enough to allow the printed fabric to hang above the boiling water.

Whatever type of steamer is employed, the printed fabric and its wrapping needs to be protected against splashes thrown up by the boiling water, condensation on the inside walls of the container and drips from above. If the fabric gets wet the print will run.

Heating may be from below (a gas ring) or, for the dustbin and larger steamers, from within by electric kettle heaters of $1\frac{1}{2}$ kilowatt capacity. The condensation will be reduced and the steam made to flow more evenly if the outside of the container is lagged. Much extra labour and the risk of the water supply boiling dry can be avoided if whenever possible the larger steamer is connected to a water supply through a ball valve or cistern so that it tops up as the water is lost in steam.

Figures 120, 121, 122, 124, 125 and 127 show a wide variety of such steamers from the double saucepan to the tall 'star' steamer.

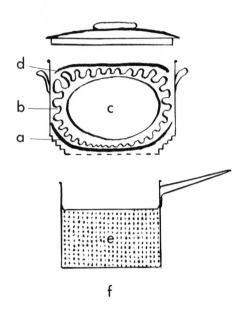

120   Vegetable Steamer. See general note on steamers.

Equipment for Double Saucepan, Cinder Sifter and Dustbin Type Steamers (Figures 120–122).

Dry steaming cloths (e.g., old sheets), a clothes horse or line, a bowl, and clean, dry newspaper, carpet underfelt and wooden tongs (which are useful for unpacking the steamer but are not essential).

121   Cinder Sifter Steamer. See general note on steamers.

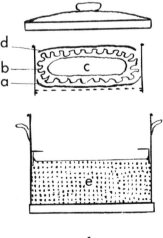

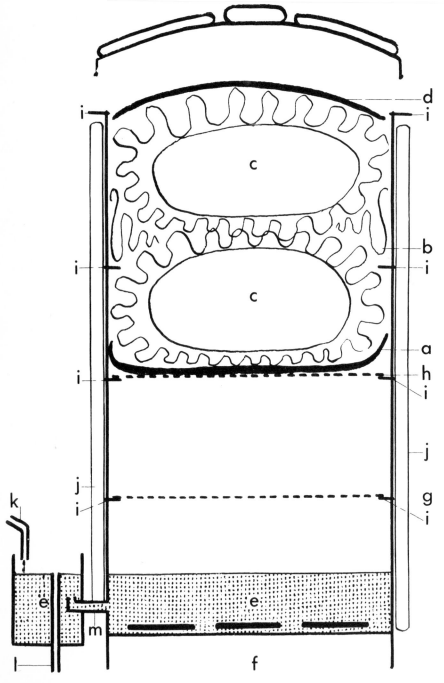

Steamers. The following key is applicable to Figures 120, 121 and 122.

a   lower piece of underfelt.
b   loosely crumpled steaming cloths.
c   wrapped fabric to be steamed.
d   top piece of underfelt.
e   water.
f   heat source for gas or electric rings; for three, 12 kilowatt, electric kettle elements; or gas rings underneath dustbin, and these additional points apply to the dustbin and star steamers.
g   loose perforated shelf of aluminium or stainless steel resting on side supports a few inches above water level which should cover heaters.
h   loose shelf of either perforated or expanded aluminium or stainless steel.
i   bolts on dustbin steamer to hold shelves and to allow steam to escape. Preferably stainless steel.
j   external lagging. For the constant level device this may either be a normal cistern or as shown.
k   from tap.
l   overflow pipe.
m   to steamer.

122   Dustbin Steamer. See general note on steamers.

Preparation

Cut 3 pieces of underfelt: 1 piece to fit the bottom of the container plus a 2 inch margin all round, a second piece to fit the perforated bottom or shelf, and the third piece to fit the *top* of the steamer.

Method

Wrapping the fabric (Figure 123). Spread out the printed fabric on a clean, *dry* table top. Cover with a single layer of *dry*, clean newspaper wider and longer than the fabric (a). Fold so that the fabric does not touch itself (b). Fold the opposite way to form a square package— 'concertina' larger pieces (c). Allow for the surrounding packing that will be required in the steamer (e.g., a dustbin type steamer will accommodate 9–10 inch squares). With a *dry* steaming cloth wrap the package (or several small ones together) into a firm—but not tight— parcel (d). Large steamers take several parcels.

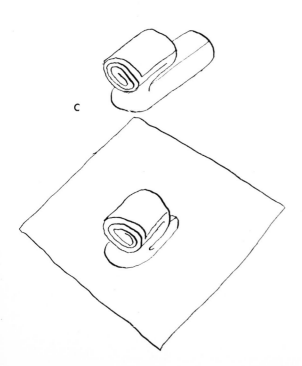

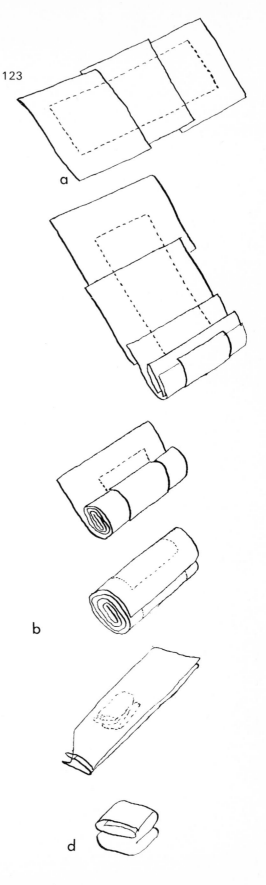

123

Packing the steamer. This must be done *quickly* and carefully. Before heating, check that the steamer contains sufficient water (e). When the steam is flowing freely, remove the lid, and pack as follows: (a) Place the underfelt flat on the base or perforated shelf, allowing the surplus to come up the sides; on this, make a loose 'nest' of steaming cloth coming up a little all round the sides (b), place the first 'parcel' in the centre of this nest, with the packing loosely bunched and the steaming cloths all round to prevent the parcel itself touching the steamer walls and so directly absorbing moisture from the sides; continue any further packing of parcels with cloths around and between (c). The last parcel must be covered with bunched cloths and a final piece or pieces of the underfelt (d). Replace the lid, and steam for the required time. *Always pack the steamer fairly loosely but right to the top.* If there is no lid to the container, place several pieces of thick underfelt supported on a frame across the top, leaving space for the steam to escape. Try to pack within a few seconds.

Star steamers are packed by rolling with steaming cloths between as in Figure 126. *Unpacking*. Do not cut off the heat before removing the parcels. Quickly shake each pad and cloth when unpacking. Remove the parcels, cut off the heat, remove the remaining cloths and underfelt. Unwrap the parcels and shake out the fabrics, place directly in cold running water and rinse very thoroughly. This is part of the fixation process and will take quite a time. It is essential to remove all the surplus dye, chemicals and gum remaining in the fabric. Do not leave the fabric soaking or the background may become stained. After this long rinse and when the rinsing water is clear, wash thoroughly as the recipe suggests.
Never leave wet prints in a heap. Squeeze gently, open out to dry, iron on the wrong side whilst damp. Spread the steaming cloths and pads out over a clothes horse to dry as soon as possible after steaming.

124

125

124/125 Star Steamer. The most expensive type of steamer and nearest to those used commercially. It can be purchased complete ready for use from such firms as Macclesfield Engineering Co. Ltd, who supply round models with a top lid (124) and square models with a front full length door (125) for easier hanging of the fabric to be steamed.

Alternatively the steamer may be made to specification in stainless steel by such a firm as G. W. Pearce and Sons Ltd, of Chester Street, Aston, Birmingham 6.

Since this type of steamer does not require folding of the printed fabric but allows it to hang and the steam to pass freely around it it is less likely to give uneven fixation.

It obtains its name from the hooked Star from which the printed fabric was suspended during steaming. This is often replaced by a piece of wooden dowelling to which the top edge of the fabric is tied with thread. The steamer should be sufficiently deep from the rod inserted at the top (n) to the loose perforated shelf (g) to allow a piece of 50-in. fabric and its wrapping to hang during steaming without touching the sides or shelf.

126 shows the printed fabric tied to the supporting rod and interleaved with steaming cloths ready to place in the steamer.

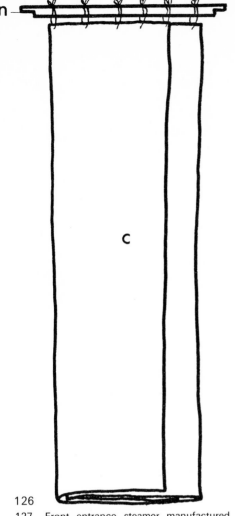

126

127 Front entrance steamer manufactured by Ashworth-Lyme Marquetry Co.

SOME FACTUAL NOTES

1 FABRIC PREPARATION

Before using any fabric, it must be well-washed to remove any impurities or dressings. These may be SIZE (added to the yarn before weaving); FILLER (added to the woven cloth to improve its feel, thickness or weight) or FINISH (such as drip-dry, non-iron, mini-care, sanforized, crease resistant, pre-shrunk, etc.). Many of these are resin-based and so very resistant to water washing. Unless you are completely certain that the fabric you wish to use is already free of impurities and/or finishes you must remove them or they may repel the dye and prevent it from reaching the fibres (this will let your dye or pattern wash or wear off in use).

The following methods may be conveniently used. Soak all fabrics (preferably overnight) in cold water.

Cotton and Linen—Boil for $\frac{1}{2}$ hour in water containing a little soapless detergent such as Stergene, Lissapol ND or Teepol (in USA, Duponol or Synthrapol).

Silk—Nearly boil (but be certain not to or you will spoil the feel and appearance of the silk) for 1 hour in a solution containing 1 part olive oil soap—10 parts of water.

Wool—Wash gently for $\frac{1}{2}$ hour in a very weak and only hand-hot solution of Stergene in water. Do NOT rub or stir in case the wool felts or hardens.

Nylon and Terylene—Soak in a weak solution of water and Lissapol ND for 30 minutes.

Rayon

VISCOSE—Boil for 30 minutes in a weak solution of water and Lissapol ND.

ACETATE—Soak for 30 minutes in a weak solution of water, Lissapol ND and a few drops of ammonia.

After scouring, all fabrics must be thoroughly rinsed in clean water and dried.

GENERAL SUPPLIERS OF MATERIALS
Great Britain
Dryad Handicrafts—Northgates, Leicester.
Margros—Monument House, Monument Way, West Woking, Surrey.
G. W. Pearce & Sons Ltd—Chester Street, Aston, Birmingham 6. Stainless steel ware.

USA
Art and Crafts Materials Corporation—321 Park Avenue, Baltimore 1, Maryland.
Craft Tools Inc.—396 Broadway, New York 13, N.Y.
School Arts Magazine publishes a directory each year in its February number listing art and craft suppliers.

SUPPLIERS OF CHEMICALS
Great Britain
Boots the Chemists—local branches will order and supply all the chemicals required in small quantities.
British Drug Houses Ltd—Poole, Dorset.
Henry Corbett Ltd—60/72 Newtown Row, Birmingham, 6 (Lissapol).
May and Baker Ltd—Dagenham, Essex.
Youngs of Leicester Ltd—40/42 Belvoir St, Leicester (also Glydote B).
Calgon—Albright and Wilson (Mfg) Ltd—1 Knightsbridge Green, London S.W.1, or local shops.
'Formosul'—Associated Chemical Companies (Sales) Ltd—PO Box 28, Beckwith, Knowle, Harrogate.
Shirlastains—Shirley Developments Ltd—Saxone House, 52/56 Market St, Manchester 1.
Lissapol D—Mayborn Products Ltd—Dylon Works, Sydenham, London S.E.6 (also related chemicals for Procion dyestuffs).

USA
Allied Chemical Corporation—General Chemical Division, PO Box 353, Morristown, New Jersey.
Berg Chemical Co.—441 West 37th St, New York, N.Y.
Calgon—Calgon Co.—271 Madison Ave, New York, N.Y.
Kromofax—Union Carbide Chemicals Co.—270 Park Avenue, New York, N.Y.

SUPPLIERS OF DYESTUFFS
Great Britain
The following are recommended:
ACID, DIRECT, PROCION M DYES in small quantities from *Candlemakers Supplies*, 101 Moore Park Road, London S.W.6.
ACID AND DIRECT DYESTUFFS—the following firms will supply small quantities.
Comak Chemicals Ltd—Swinton Works, Moon Street, London N.1.
Skilbeck Bros. Ltd—55 Glengall Road, London S.E.15.
Pronk Davis and Rusby Ltd—44 Penton Street, London N.1.
Basil Hollobon—67 Skipton Road, Ilkley, Yorkshire.
The following firms supply only larger quantities:—
Ciba Clayton Ltd—Clayton, Manchester 11.
Imperial Chemical Industries—Dyehouse Department, Manchester 9.
REACTIVE DYESTUFFS—Cibacrons in small quantities. Albegal C, Catalyst CCI in minimum 2 lb. lots from *H. Christian Ltd*—62 New Walk, Leicester, LE1 6TF.
PROCION M (COLD) AND H (HOT) REACTIVE DYESTUFFS
Both these classes of dyestuffs and their related chemicals are retailed in small and large quantities by:
Mayborn Products Ltd—Dylon Works, Sydenham, London S.E.26.

The Procions in larger quantities, are also obtainable from:

Skilbeck Bros. Ltd—55 Glengall Road, London S.E.15.

Imperial Chemical Industries—Dyestuffs Department, Manchester 9.

Reactive dyestuffs are also obtainable from Basil Hollobon, 67 Skipton Road, Ilkley, Yorkshire.

PIGMENT COLOURS

Fabricol—Margros, Monument House, Monument Way West, Woking, Surrey.

Polyprint Pigment dyestuffs. M. E. Mc-Creary & Co.—Polyprint, 815 Lisburn Road, Belfast, BT9 7GX.

Printex Pigment dyestuffs (originally called Tinolite). *Winsor and Newton Ltd*—Wealdstone, Harrow, Middlesex.

Tri Chem—Tri Chem Ltd—Victoria Laboratories, Shuttleworth Road, Goldington, Bedford—packed in ball point marker type holders, useful for line drawing on hangings.

PRINTING INKS—fine fabric printing inks in tubes and Thinners.

T. N. Lawrence & Son Ltd—Bleeding Heart Yard, Greville Street, London E.C.1.

DYLON COLD and HOT WATER DYES and DYGON—In small and large quantities—

Mayborn Products Ltd—Dylon Works, Sydenham, London S.E.26.

Most chemists, hardware and department stores also stock Dylons.

USA

Aco-Lite Pigment colors and binders—American Crayon Co., Sandusky, Ohio.

Acid and Direct dyestuffs—ICI Organics Inc., 55 Canal Street, Providence, Rhode Island.

Aquaprint colors—Interchem, New Jersey.

Helizarin Pigment dyestuffs—American Cyanamid Co., Dyes Division, Princeton, New Jersey.

Prang Aqua Pigment Textile colors—The American Crayon Co., Sandusky, Ohio.

Procion Reactive dyestuffs—*Arnold, Hoffman & Co. Inc.,* 55 Canal St, Providence, Rhode Island and *Chemical Manufacturing Co.* Madison Avenue, New York, N.Y.

Reactone Reactive and Tinolite Pigment dyestuffs—Geigy Chemical Co., PO Box 430, Yonkers, New York.

SUPPLIERS OF FABRICS FOR PRINTING

The following firms will supply fabrics often ready for printing, against official orders or cash with the order. (This includes carriage on small quantities.) Ask for the current prices and samples before ordering. Test the sample before commencing upon the piece of work.

Great Britain

COTTONS, LINENS, RAYONS

Emil Adler—46 Mortimer Street, London W.1, for inexpensive fine lawns and cottons.

R. V. Bailey & Co. Ltd—62 Mina Road, Bristol—suppliers of white calico for dyeing and printing

Bradleys—Stott Street, Nelson, Lancs., for calicos, cottons and rayons.

Dryad Handicrafts—Northgates, Leicester have for many years provided a comprehensive range of fabrics (including rayons) for all textile work. Their current materials include many ready for printing. Where a fabric is required for use with dyes, as distinct from pigments, enquiry should be made as to whether it contains any dressing or is prepared ready for printing or dyeing.

Edinburgh Weavers—Nelson Street, Carlisle, are suppliers of white cotton cloths of varying textures prepared ready for printing. Those usually available include plain cottons, bark cotton (a textured material) and cotton satin, all 50 inches wide.

These manufacturers pioneered this service to schools and colleges against official orders for half (30 yards) and full pieces (60 yards) at reasonable prices.

Joshua Hoyle—50 Piccadilly, Manchester 1, for bleached, plain calico in pieces (100 yards).

Thomas Mason Ltd—Sales Division, Primet Mills, Colne, Lancs. Mercerized cotton.

M. E. McCreary & Co.—21 Prince Edward Drive, Belfast 9, Northern Ireland, sell 36 inch wide cotton bleached and prepared for printing in any length from 5 yards upwards (supplies also of Polyprint pigment dyestuffs).

A. Nadler Ltd—Commercial Street, Knott Mill, Manchester 15, suppliers of cheap but very satisfactory bleached and unbleached pillow cotton, calico and other fabrics in many widths and supplied in any length from 10 yards upwards.

Stott and Smith—173 Plymouth Grove, Manchester, 13—for cheap bleached cottons.

Tootal Thompson Fabrics—Dept 12/2, P.O. Box 119, Wiltom House, Whitworth Street West, Manchester 1, 35/36 inch white, shrunk, mercerized fabric, Ref B/MS, in half or full (120 yard) pieces.

Whitworth and Mitchell Ltd—Wemco Fabrics, 15 Cross Street, Manchester 2, supply an excellent and reasonably priced mercerized cotton, 36 inches, (Ref PS 322X) in piece length as well as other mercerised poplin and cotton fabrics.

SILKS

Emil Adler—46 Mortimer Street, London W.1, for inexpensive 36-inch silk.

Coles, Son and Co. Ltd—25/26 Dering Street, New Bond Street, London W.1, supply a number of suitable silks in piece lengths.

Dryad Handicrafts—Northgates, Leicester carry a useful 36-inch white silk foulard obtainable in any length.

Pongees Ltd—Empire House, St Martins-Le-Grand, London E.C.1, are one of the very few firms, perhaps the last, who can still supply a wide range of qualities at reasonable prices suitable for printing without any de-gumming process. Orders are accepted for half and full pieces (a full piece is between 45 and 55 yards).

USA
COTTONS, LINENS ETC.

Fabric Distributing Co.—545/551 Eighth Avenue, New York, N.Y., for cotton fabrics prepared for dyeing and printing and also organdie for screen covering.

Imperial Linens Inc.—302 Fifth Avenue, New York, N.Y., for scoured linen.

SUPPLIERS OF THICKENERS
Great Britain

Manutex—Alginate Industries Ltd—22 Henrietta St, London W.C.2.

Nafka—Gordon Slater Ltd—Crown St, Chester Rd, Manchester 15.

USA

Halltex—Stein Hall & Co. Inc.—605 Third Avenue, New York, N.Y.

Keltex—Kelco Co.—75 Terminal Ave, Clark, New Jersey.

BOOKSELLERS
Specializing in books on Crafts and particularly Textiles.

Great Britain

F. Lewis, Publishers Ltd—The Tithe House, 1461 London Road, Leigh-on-Sea. An outstanding publisher of books on textiles and other art subjects. Many excellent series, including 'A Survey of World Textiles' (1 volume per country). They are also official representatives of many foreign specialist publishers.

K. R. Drummond—30 Hart Grove, Ealing Common, London W.5, is the only specialist shop as far as we know which, although stocking and obtaining and selling all new and secondhand books on Arts and Crafts in their widest sense, also specializes in Textiles and produces admirable catalogues.

Foyles Bookshop, Charing Cross Road, London.

T. N. Lawrence & Son Ltd—2/4 Bleeding Heart Yard, London E.C.1.

Messrs Luzac of Great Russell Street, London, (particularly for Indian and Far East textiles).

Tiranti Bookshop—72 Charlotte Street, London W.1.

Zwemmers Bookshop—Charing Cross Road, London.

Victoria and Albert Museum—South Kensington, London S.W.7, (or H. M. Stationery Offices). A variety of handbooks on such topics as William Morris, Embroidery, Printed textiles, etc.

USA

Perkins Oriental Books—255 Seventh Avenue, New York.

Charles E. Tuttle Co.—Rutland, Vermont & Tokyo, Japan.

Creative Hands Bookshop—Printers Building, Worcester, Mass.

The Unicorn—Books for craftsmen, Box 645C, Rockville, Maryland.

Museum Books Inc.—48 East 43rd Street, New York, N.Y.

LIBRARIES with good sections on textiles
Great Britain
—London
The British Museum, Great Russell Street.
Victoria and Albert Museum, South Kensington.
Design Centre, Haymarket.
All carry specialist libraries on textiles.

—Provincial
Bradford, Glasgow, Leeds, Manchester Libraries all have good textile sections in their collections.
Bawthorpe Hall—Burnley has a library and special student facilities.

USA
Museum of Modern Art Library—11 West 53rd Street, N.Y. 19.

PAPER PATTERNS for small articles, dolls' clothes, hats, bags, ties etc. are published by Buttericks, McCalls and Simplicity.

PHOTOGRAPHS AND TRANSPARENCIES OF TEXTILES

Great Britain
The British Museum, Victoria and Albert Museum and *The Design Centre* will all supply black and white photographs to order at varying prices (depending upon the size) of the items in their collections. One may also photograph exhibits by arrangement with the museum.
The Miniature Gallery—60 Rushett Close, Long Ditton, Surrey, supply many sets and single transparencies of an exceedingly high standard of all types of textiles. They issue very full catalogues and are agents in this country for transparencies prepared by Dr Block of Hollywood, California. These cover many crafts, both historic and contemporary and include a large number of textiles.
Educational Productions Ltd—17 Denbigh Street, London S.W.1.
Visual Publications Ltd—197 Kensington High Street, London W.8.
Diana Wylie Ltd—3 Park Road, London N.W.1.
Pictorial Colour Slides—242 Langley Way, West Wickham, Kent.

The Education Division, GB Instructional Ltd—Imperial House, 80/82 Regent Street, London W.1.
Looking and Seeing (Filmstrips)—81 Southway, London N.20
All these firms produce filmstrips and/or transparencies some of which are of textiles.

USA

Dr Block Color Productions—1309 North Genesee Avenue, Hollywood 46, California. Publish some of the finest textile transparencies available.
Bailey Films Inc—6509 De Longre Avenue, Hollywood, California.

USEFUL JOURNALS (including articles on textiles and/or design)

Craft Publications

Craft Horizons published bi-monthly by the American Craftsmen's Council, 44 West 53rd Street, N.Y. 19, N.Y., USA. Unusually well-illustrated articles.
Design published monthly by Council of Industrial Design, The Design Centre, 28 Haymarket, London S.W.1.
The Journal of the Society of Dyers and Colourists published monthly by the Society Dean House, Piccadilly, Bradford, Yorks, England.
Textile History published annually by David & Charles, South Devon House, Railway Station, Newton Abbot, Devon.
BBC Pamphlets for Radio and Television series are often a fruitful source of ideas for layout and design.
Handweaver and Craftsman published quarterly from 220 Fifth Avenue, New York, USA.

Teaching Publications

Everyday Art—a free publication each quarter from The American Crayon Co., Sandusky, Ohio, USA, upon children's art and crafts. Noted for its original layout, ideas and freedom from publishers' advertising.

School Arts—Davis Publications Inc., Printers' Building, Worcester, Mass, USA. A lively publication with many well-illustrated articles on the theory and practice of education through art and crafts.
Art and Craft Education—Evans Brothers, Montague House, Russell Square, London W.C.1. A useful monthly which often carries articles on textiles in school.

Trade and General Interest Publications

American Fabrics Magazine—Reporter Publications Inc., N.Y., USA. Quarterly
Fashion and Fabrics—USA.
Drapery and Fashion Weekly—NTP Business Journal, 40 Bowling Green Lane, London E.C.1. A Trade paper with useful specialist articles and supplements on new fabrics, fashions and techniques.
Ambassador British Export journal for fabric fashions. Monthly
Domus (Italy) Monthly
Harpers' Bazaar Monthly
House Beautiful USA Monthly
House and Garden Monthly
Interiors Monthly
Vogue Monthly and special numbers
International Textiles Amsterdam. Fashions, fabrics and men's wear. Monthly
Modern Textiles USA. Specializing in rayon and synthetic fibres. Monthly
L'Art et La Mode French. Haute couture fashions. Expensive. Two-monthly
Franks Fashion Guide published by R. D. Franks Ltd, Kent House, Market Place, Oxford Circus, London W.1, is a useful booklet listing Fashion Magazines from all over the world, Technical Books and Workroom Equipment for all forms of dressmaking. Annual

TRADE AND PROFESSIONAL ORGANIZATIONS OFFERING EDUCATIONAL MATERIAL AND ADVICE ON TEXTILES

Association of British Launderers and Cleaners Ltd—16/17 Lancaster Gate, London W.2 (Amalgamated with the National Federation of Dyers and Cleaners).

British Carpet Centre—Dorland House, 14/16 Regent Street, London S.W.1.

British Man-Made Fibres Federation—Bridgewater House, 58 Whitworth Street, Manchester 1. (Free booklet on 'Facts about man-made Fibres'.)

British Wool Marketing Board—Kew Bridge House, Kew Bridge Road, Brentford, Middlesex. (Literature and wall-charts for sale.)

The Textile Council (formerly The Cotton Board)—12 Great Marlborough Street, London W.1.
(Free Literature and catalogue on booklets and sample box of cotton from ball to fabric available at part cost.)

The Cotton, Silk and Man-Made Fibres Research Association—Shirley Institute, Didsbury, Manchester 20.

Design Centre—28 Haymarket, London S.W.1.

The Flaxspinners and Manufacturers' Association of Great Britain—Public Relations Officer, 4 Chamber of Commerce Buildings, Dundee. (Flax/linen educational box available at part cost.)

International Wool Secretariat, UK Branch, Dept. of Education and Training, Wool House, Carlton Gardens, London S.W.1.

The Irish Linen Guild—Morley House, 314 Regent Street, London W.1.

The Silk Centre—Dorland House, 18/20 Regent Street, London S.W.1. (Leaflets and samples at nominal charges, Teachers' set 4s. 0d., Students' set 1s. 6d.)

The Silk and Man-Made Fibre Users Association—Dorland House, 18/20 Regent Street, London S.W.1.

Joseph Bancroft and Sons Co. (England) Ltd—134 Wigmore Street, London W.1. (Free leaflets on choice and use of lace and lace patterns.)

Proban Ltd—34 Princess Street, Manchester 1. (Free leaflets and sample fabric strips available, small charge for large quantities.)

DuPont Company (UK) Ltd—DuPont House, 18 Bream's Buildings, Fetter Lane, London E.C.4. (Free leaflets on Orlon, Dacron, Lycrol and DuPont Nylon.)

Monsanto Textiles Ltd—11 King Richard's Road, Leicester, LE3 5QB. (Free leaflets on Acrilan and Blue 'C' Nylon.)

The Calico Printers' Association Ltd—Publicity Dept, St James Buildings, Oxford Street, Manchester 1. (Free booklet and samples of Calpreta permanent finishes.)

MUSEUMS AND CENTRES WITH COLLECTIONS OF TEXTILES
EUROPE
Great Britain
CONTEMPORARY examples in current production

Design Centre—28 Haymarket, London S.W.1—a permanent but constantly changing exhibition of well-designed modern British goods in current production including printed and woven textiles.

Crafts Centre of Great Britain—43 Earlham Street, Covent Garden, London W.C.2 —exhibitions and sales by craftsmen including textile designers and makers.

Crafts Council of Great Britain—47 Victoria Street, London S.W.1—an association of craftsmen holding regular exhibitions.

The Textile Council (formerly The Cotton Board)—3 Alberton Street, Manchester 3 —changing exhibitions particularly of design as applied to textiles.

The Bladon Gallery—Hurstbourne Tarrant, Andover, Hants.—a society of craftsmen who exhibit and sell in these galleries a wide range of craftwork including textiles.

Bluecoat Display Centre—50 Bluecoat Chambers, School Lane, Liverpool 1—a similar organization.

The Society of Craftsmen—Old Kemble Galleries, 29 Church Street, Hereford—a similar organization.

HISTORIC examples in piece, length and made up into costumes, etc.

The British Museum—Great Russell Street, London W.C.1—outstanding collections of nineteenth-century textiles from West Africa and the Near East. Particularly the Charles Beving collection of West African tie dye and starch resist fabrics in the Ethnographical department.

The Victoria and Albert Museum—South Kensington, London S.W.7—the finest collections of textiles (in length and costume) in the British Isles. Particularly the Department of Textiles where the primary collection in the Textiles Study Rooms contains a representative selection of embroidered, printed and woven textiles. Serious students may study further in the reserve collections which are among the most comprehensive in the world and include such items as the Aurel Stein collection from Khotan. Do not be misled by the museum's title, exhibits from all periods and countries are available backed by an exceptionally well-informed and co-operative staff.

Housed within the V & A is the Indian Section (once the India Museum) which is a self-contained department containing a superb collection of Indian culture and particularly Indian textiles of all kinds.

The Circulation department contains, amongst much art and crafts material, many examples and photographs of contemporary and older textiles which are available on loan to approved establishments.

NOTE: Permission to see reserved collections in both these museums should be obtained by applying in writing to the keeper of the appropriate department, stating exact details of the facilities required.

Bethnal Green Museum—Cambridge Heath Road, London E.2—costumes, Spitalfield silks and other items such as rare dolls' houses, English silver etc.

Horniman Museum—London Road, Forest Hill, London S.E.23—an excellently arranged ethnographical museum of man, his arts, crafts etc.

William Morris Gallery (and Brangwyn Gift), Lloyd Park, Walthamstow, London E.17—an interesting collection of Morris' original designs and examples of his craftsmanship.

The Folio Society—6 Stratford Place, London W.1—is a society whose members may purchase antiques and curios at their gallery, pieces of historic textiles are often available.

Eaton, Manette Street, London (between Foyles' Bookshops) sells original contemporary printed tapa or bark cloth from the South Seas.

The Whitworth Art Gallery—Manchester —a most interesting and comprehensive collection.

The Pitt Rivers Museum—University of Oxford—an interesting ethnographical collection.

Lewis Textile Museum—Blackburn—particularly of spinning and weaving.

Bawthorpe Hall—Burnley—large collection, library and special facilities for students.

Bankfield Museum—Halifax—machinery and textiles.

Lullingstone Silk Farm—Ayot House, Ayot St Lawrence, Herts.—only silk farm in the country where visitors, including school parties, may see all the stages of silk production.

Museums and Galleries in Great Britain and Ireland is published annually by Index Publishers, 27/28 Finsbury Square, London E.C.2. It contains a list of places with Textile collections as well as full information upon most museums in the British Isles.

USA

Textile Museum—Washington.

Smithsonian Institute

The American Museum of Natural History—New York.

Metropolitan Museum of Art—New York.

Cooper Union Museum—New York.

Museum of the American Indian

Brooklyn Museum Collection

Bertha Schaefer Gallery—New York.

Yale University

A. S. Kohler Collection—Ascona.

STORES & SHOPS

Most large department stores carry stocks of printed textiles but outstanding amongst the London stores are:

Sandersons of Berners Street, textiles and wallpapers superbly displayed.

Heals of Tottenham Court Road, textiles, furniture etc.

Liberty's of Regent Street, textiles etc.

Habitat of Tottenham Court Road, and other cities.

Conran of Tottenham Court Road.

Certain textile printing firms welcome visitors at prearranged times. For details write to such firms as:

Sandersons, London (also wallpapers).

David Whitehead, Rawtenstall.

Fergusons, Carlisle.

Edinburgh Weavers, Carlisle.

Hull Traders, Hull.

SOCIETIES CATERING FOR TEXTILE PRINTERS
Great Britain

Association of Guilds of Weavers, Spinners and Dyers

(Regional Guilds also meet in various parts of the country) Hon. Secretary: Miss Mary Blair, Greengate, Tarporley, Cheshire.

The Society for Education Through Art

This society furthers the cause of Arts and Crafts in all types of schools and colleges. It works centrally in London and through Regional Groups. It holds conferences, refresher courses, lectures. Publishes 'Athene' and a Bulletin and circulates portfolios of children's work. Enquiries to the Secretary, SEA, 29 Great James Street, London W.C.1, enclose s.a.e.

Society of Dyers and Colourists—32/34 Piccadilly, Bradford, Yorks.

Textile Institute—16 St Mary's Parsonage, Manchester 3.

The 62 Group—Secretary, 59 Belmont Park, London S.E.13. A group to promote and encourage the high standard of work by embroidery designers and craftsmen which they consider necessary for the survival of embroidery. Exhibits and sells collage and embroidery.

Textile Council—12 Great Marlborough Street, London W.1.

COURSES FOR TEXTILE PRINTERS

There are many courses and summer schools held throughout the country by local Education Authorities and private bodies. These offer classes or groups in varying textile techniques. Unfortunately it is becoming increasingly difficult to find practical courses in colleges of Art for the home craftsman or teacher not wishing to take a Diploma course.

We would recommend the following:

Great Britain

1. The excellent practical courses at Dartington conducted by Susan Bosence and Annette Kok, on dyeing and printing techniques (including batik, tie and dye, natural dyes etc.) which take place during vacations. For details of these and others held by various Guilds of Craftsmen write to the Warden, Devon Centre for Further Education, Dartington College of Arts, Totnes, Devon (Totnes 2267).

2. The annual summer school held by the Association of Guilds of Weavers, Spinners and Dyers at different places in England and the regular meetings held by the many regional guilds of this Association. The honorary secretary, Miss Mary Blair, Greengate, Tarporley, Cheshire will supply full details and the address of your nearest guild secretary.

3. The annual Cardiff Summer schools (write to the Cardiff Education Authority for details) have extensive sections on decorative textile constructions and other techniques.

USA

Craft Horizons—issued bi-monthly by the American Craftsmen's Council, 16 East 52nd Street, New York, N.Y., carries regular supplements with details of courses and schools held throughout the different states. It also issues an annual Crafts Courses Directory obtainable from the Publications Department, ACC, 29 West 53rd Street, New York, N.Y. 10019.

Textile Crafts—a guide book to textile handicraft courses, 856N, Genesee, Los Angeles, California.

Handweaver and Craftsman—issued quarterly from 10 McGovern Avenue, Lancaster, Pa.—carries details of summer courses.

A SELECTED BIBLIOGRAPHY

General technical and source books on Fabric Printing of all types:

An Introduction to Textile Printing—ICI and Butterworths, London, 1967 (revised). A comprehensive and practical handbook covering block and screen, discharge and Batik on a variety of fibres and the appropriate dyestuffs required.

Dyes and Dyeing by P. Gilmour, Society for Education Through Art, London, 1967. A most useful and inexpensive booklet with many recipes.

Colour and Texture in Creative Textile Craft by R. Hartung, Batsford, London, 1965.
Very good ideas for individual experimenting.

Textile Printing and Dyeing by N. Proud, Batsford, London, 1965.
Simply written on basic techniques.

Introducing Dyeing and Printing by B. Ash and T. Dyson, Batsford, London, 1970.

Fabric Printing by Hand by S. Russ, Studio Vista, London, 1964.
A well-illustrated and practical handbook.

Textiles in the Home by Rankin and Hildreth, Allman, London, 1966.
A most useful book containing a great deal of practical information.

Designing with String by M. Seyd, Batsford, London, 1967.
A most original and inspiring book.

A History of Dyed Textiles by Stuart Robinson, Studio Vista, London, 1969.

A History of Printed Textiles by Stuart Robinson, Studio Vista, London, 1969.
Both books contain exhaustive bibliographies on the history of textiles.

INDEX INCLUDING A LIST OF ILLUSTRATIONS

Bold numbers refer to illustrations